CHILDREN'S ISSUES, LAWS AND PROGRAM

CHILD SUPPORT ISSUES

FEDERAL POLICY ON MEDICAL CARE AND INCARCERATION AS AN ENFORCEMENT TOOL

RENE PELLERIN
EDITOR

NOVINKA

New York

Library of Congress Cataloging-in-Publication Data

ISBN: 978-1-62808-376-7

Published by Nova Science Publishers, Inc. † New York

CONTENTS

PREFACE

The Child Support Enforcement (CSE) program was signed into law in 1975 as a federal-state program to enhance the well-being of families by making child support a reliable source of income. The CSE program is based on the premise that both parents are financially responsible for their children. The CSE program is operated in all 50 states, the District of Columbia, Guam, Puerto Rico, and the U.S. Virgin Islands, and by several Indian tribes or tribal organizations. State CSE programs have at their disposal a wide variety of methods by which to obtain child support obligations. In addition, states under their own authority and the authority of their courts can use the threat of incarceration and/or actual incarceration. This book provides an overview on federal policies relating to medical care and incarceration as an enforcement tool in child support cases. Included in this book also are frequently asked questions relating to child custody and support issues.

Chapter 1 - Medical child support is defined as the legal provision of payment of medical, dental, prescription, and other health care expenses for children living apart from one of their parents. It can include provisions for health care coverage (including payment of costs of premiums, co- payments, and deductibles) as well as cash payments for a child's medical expenses. The establishment and enforcement of medical support is intended to promote fairness in allocating childrearing costs between custodial and noncustodial parents and, when employer-sponsored health care is obtained, it saves federal and state dollars.

Medical child support has evolved over time. In the early days of the establishment and enforcement of medical child support, the primary goal was to make noncustodial parents responsible for their children and thereby lessen taxpayer burden by shifting costs to noncustodial parents. With the enactment of P.L. 109-171 (the Deficit Reduction Act of 2005), the emphasis on solely looking to the noncustodial parent for obtaining private health care coverage for children was replaced with the view that provision of medical child support is the goal regardless of which parent can provide it.

A study was commissioned by the Department of Health and Human Services (HHS), and conducted by the Urban Institute, to shed light on health care coverage of child support-eligible children. Based on an analysis using 2008 data, the Urban Institute found that out of an estimated 26 million U.S. children age 18 or under who had at least one parent living outside the home, approximately 51% of such child support-eligible children were enrolled in the Medicaid or the State Children's Health Insurance Program (CHIP). An additional 31% of the child support- eligible population had private coverage from someone in their household and 6% obtained insurance coverage from someone outside the household (generally the noncustodial parent but sometimes a stepparent). A small proportion of children (1%) obtained coverage from other federal sources. The remaining 11% of child support-eligible children were classified as uninsured.

Health care coverage of children and medical child support are not synonymous. A child could be covered by a custodial parent's health insurance plan and the child support order may not contain any provision for medical support. Conversely, a child may be receiving cash medical support but not be insured.

Although there is agreement that many children still lack health care coverage, full implementation of the Patient Protection and Affordable Care Act (P.L. 111-148; ACA, as amended) should further reduce the problem of uninsured children, but the issue of successful establishment and enforcement of medical child support may become even more complex. Although states submit medical support data to the federal government, the information is not subject to an audit to determine if it is complete and reliable. Also, medical support establishment allows states to initiate legal medical support orders before determining whether or not health insurance is affordable. However, state Child Support Enforcement (CSE) agencies are severely hampered, if not totally stymied, in enforcing medical child support orders in cases in which a medical support order is established but the health insurance is not considered affordable by federal/state standards.

Even though it is not likely that medical child support will receive congressional attention this year, with the continued implementation of the ACA in 2014, Congress may examine the impact of the ACA on the CSE program and address unresolved issues. This report describes current federal policy with respect to medical child support. It also examines the potential impact of the ACA on the CSE program. It provides a legislative history of medical support provisions in the CSE program and state data on the medical support coverage of children in the CSE program.

Chapter 2 - The Child Support Enforcement (CSE) program was signed into law in 1975 (P.L. 93-647) as a federal-state program to enhance the well-being of families by making child support a reliable source of income. The CSE program is based on the premise that both parents are financially responsible for their children. The CSE program is operated in all 50 states, the District of Columbia, Guam, Puerto Rico, and the U.S. Virgin Islands, and by several Indian tribes or tribal organizations. State CSE programs have at their disposal a wide variety of methods by which to obtain child support obligations. In addition, states under their own authority and the authority of their courts can use the threat of incarceration and/or actual incarceration.

Nonpayment of support may subject a noncustodial parent to criminal sanctions in three situations: (1) a finding of contempt of court for failure to obey a court's child support order, (2) prosecution under a state criminal nonsupport statute, or (3) prosecution under federal criminal penalties for nonpayment of child support. Contempt of court is classified as either "civil" or "criminal." Civil contempt occurs when an individual willfully disobeys a court order or rule. Criminal contempt occurs when an individual interferes with the ability of the court to function properly. Judges can sentence individuals to imprisonment upon a finding of contempt.

Many contend that the incarceration of persons for nonpayment of child support is both wrong and counterproductive. They say that criminalizing nonpayment of child support by making it a misdemeanor and/or felony disproportionately affects low-income noncustodial parents who more likely than not are just as poor or poorer than the mother and children owed child support payments. They assert that incarceration means that the noncustodial parent is not working and earning money and that having a criminal record lowers a person's job prospects. They also contend that the negative ramifications of being in jail include a weakened bond between the noncustodial parent and his or her children and family and a high probability that the individual will ultimately be re-incarcerated for nonpayment of child support or other infractions or crimes.

Others say that for some noncustodial parents, the threat of being incarcerated for nonpayment of support is not enough. For these persons, they say that incarceration is necessary. They contend that some noncustodial parents would rather quit their jobs, go from job to job, work in the underground economy (where earnings are not reported to anyone), or engage in illegal activity rather than meet their child support obligations. They argue that child support is a source of income that could mean the difference between poverty and self-sufficiency for some families. They say that children ought not to be short-changed because of recalcitrant noncustodial parents, and maintain that nonpayment of child support is a real crime and should be treated as such.

Using jail as an option for nonpayment of child support has many implications: Are low-income noncustodial parents who are unable to fulfill their child support obligations penalized for being poor? Should noncustodial parents charged with civil contempt of court be entitled to an attorney? Should noncustodial parents whose only offense is nonpayment of child support be incarcerated in settings known to be violent and dangerous? Should incarcerating noncustodial parents be eliminated as an option due to the high costs associated with incarceration? This report includes an Appendix that indicates that all 50 states and the District of Columbia have criminal penalties for nonpayment of child support. Table A-1 shows state statute citations and the maximum penalties associated with nonpayment of child support.

Chapter 3 - The national Census Bureau data show that in 2009, nearly 13.7 million parents had custody of children under age 21 while the other parent lived elsewhere, and the aggregate amount of child support received was $21.4 billion. In 2009, 82% of custodial parents were mothers. Of all custodial parents, 52% were white, 25% were black, 19% were Hispanic, 18% were married, 34% were divorced, 35% were never married, 15% did not have a high school diploma, 17% had at least a bachelor's degree, 50% worked full-time year-round, 28% had family income below poverty, and 38% received some type of public assistance. In 2009, only 2.4 million (35%) of the 6.9 million custodial parents with child support orders actually received the full amount of child support that was owed to them. The average yearly child support payment received by custodial parents with payments was $5,248 for mothers and $4,202 for fathers. These full or partial payments represented 17% of the custodial mothers' total yearly income and 10% of the custodial fathers'. Compared to 1993 Census data, less child support was received by custodial parents in 2009 ($22.8 billion in 1993 versus $21.4 billion in 2009; in 2009 dollars). However, a higher percentage of those owed child support actually received all that they were due (36.9% in 1993 versus 41.2% in 2009).

Chapter 4 - Under the U.S. Constitution, Congress has little direct authority to legislate in the field of domestic relations. Generally, state policy guides these decisions.

Despite the lack of direct authority to legislate domestic relations issues, Congress continues to enact federal laws that indirectly affect family law questions concerning child custody and support. This report answers questions frequently asked regarding the interplay between federal and state laws governing these areas.

In: Child Support Issues
Editor: Rene Pellerin
ISBN: 978-1-62808-376-7

Chapter 1

MEDICAL CHILD SUPPORT: BACKGROUND AND CURRENT POLICY*

Carmen Solomon-Fears

SUMMARY

Medical child support is defined as the legal provision of payment of medical, dental, prescription, and other health care expenses for children living apart from one of their parents. It can include provisions for health care coverage (including payment of costs of premiums, co- payments, and deductibles) as well as cash payments for a child's medical expenses. The establishment and enforcement of medical support is intended to promote fairness in allocating childrearing costs between custodial and noncustodial parents and, when employer-sponsored health care is obtained, it saves federal and state dollars.

Medical child support has evolved over time. In the early days of the establishment and enforcement of medical child support, the primary goal was to make noncustodial parents responsible for their children and thereby lessen taxpayer burden by shifting costs to noncustodial parents. With the enactment of P.L. 109-171 (the Deficit Reduction Act of 2005), the emphasis on solely looking to the noncustodial parent for obtaining private health care coverage for children was replaced with the view that provision of medical child support is the goal regardless of which parent can provide it.

---

* This is an edited, reformatted and augmented version of the Congressional Research Service Publication, CRS Report for Congress R43020, dated March 21, 2013.

A study was commissioned by the Department of Health and Human Services (HHS), and conducted by the Urban Institute, to shed light on health care coverage of child support-eligible children. Based on an analysis using 2008 data, the Urban Institute found that out of an estimated 26 million U.S. children age 18 or under who had at least one parent living outside the home, approximately 51% of such child support-eligible children were enrolled in the Medicaid or the State Children's Health Insurance Program (CHIP). An additional 31% of the child support- eligible population had private coverage from someone in their household and 6% obtained insurance coverage from someone outside the household (generally the noncustodial parent but sometimes a stepparent). A small proportion of children (1%) obtained coverage from other federal sources. The remaining 11% of child support-eligible children were classified as uninsured.

Health care coverage of children and medical child support are not synonymous. A child could be covered by a custodial parent's health insurance plan and the child support order may not contain any provision for medical support. Conversely, a child may be receiving cash medical support but not be insured.

Although there is agreement that many children still lack health care coverage, full implementation of the Patient Protection and Affordable Care Act (P.L. 111-148; ACA, as amended) should further reduce the problem of uninsured children, but the issue of successful establishment and enforcement of medical child support may become even more complex. Although states submit medical support data to the federal government, the information is not subject to an audit to determine if it is complete and reliable. Also, medical support establishment allows states to initiate legal medical support orders before determining whether or not health insurance is affordable. However, state Child Support Enforcement (CSE) agencies are severely hampered, if not totally stymied, in enforcing medical child support orders in cases in which a medical support order is established but the health insurance is not considered affordable by federal/state standards.

Even though it is not likely that medical child support will receive congressional attention this year, with the continued implementation of the ACA in 2014, Congress may examine the impact of the ACA on the CSE program and address unresolved issues. This report describes current federal policy with respect to medical child support. It also examines the potential impact of the ACA on the CSE program. It provides a legislative history of medical support provisions in the CSE program (see **Appendix A**) and state data on the medical support coverage of children in the CSE program (see **Appendix B)**.

BACKGROUND

Many Americans view health care for their children and themselves as one of their top concerns.[1] The adverse consequences of going without health insurance may include unmet health and dental needs, lower receipt of preventive services, avoidable hospitalizations, increased likelihood of receiving expensive emergency room care, and reduced likelihood that the doctor is familiar with the patient's medical history. From a public health perspective, early and frequent monitoring of children's health is a key component to ensuring the appropriate growth and development of children. From a family perspective, health insurance coverage can reduce parental financial and emotional stress.

Child support is the cash payment that noncustodial parents are obligated to pay to custodial parents for the financial support of their children. Child support payments enable parents who do not live with their children to fulfill their financial obligation to their children by contributing to the payment of childrearing costs.

Ensuring that children get health care is one of the basic responsibilities of the Child Support Enforcement (CSE) program.[2] Operating under federal and state statutes and regulations, state and local child support agencies are required to ensure that health care costs, generally referred to as medical support,[3] are included in every child support order. These costs may include payment of medical, dental, prescription and other health care expenses for children and provisions to cover health insurance costs as well as cash payments for unreimbursed medical expenses. State child support guidelines, as well as state law and guidance, operationalize what constitutes medical support in a particular state.[4] This broad definition of medical support is relatively recent. Originally, federal requirements for child support orders focused on reimbursement for Medicaid expenses and employer-related health insurance available to the noncustodial parent.

Beginning in 1977, Congress has tried to offset some of the state costs associated with the Medicaid program (Title XIX of the Social Security Act) by allowing states to require Medicaid recipients to assign their child support rights to the state and allowing the state to pursue private health insurance coverage and/or noncustodial parents for reimbursement of the cost of Medicaid benefits provided to the child. The underlying assumption was that children enrolled in public health coverage (i.e., Medicaid) might obtain employer-based coverage (to offset the cost of Medicaid) through the noncustodial parent. Beginning in 1984, mandatory assignment became law.

In 1984, federal law required that state CSE agencies petition for the inclusion of medical support as part of any child support order whenever health care coverage was available to the noncustodial parent at reasonable cost. A 1993 amendment to the Employee Retirement Income Security Act (ERISA) required employer-sponsored group health plans to extend health care coverage to the children of a parent/employee who is divorced, separated, or never married when ordered to do so by the state CSE agency via a Qualified Medical Child Support Order (QMCSO). The 1996 welfare reform law further strengthened medical support by stipulating that all orders enforced by the state CSE agency must include a provision for health care coverage. The 1996 law also directed the CSE agency to notify the noncustodial parent's employer of the employee's medical child support obligation.[5] To help obtain health care coverage for children, a 1998 law authorized the creation of the National Medical Support Notice (NMSN), a standardized form that is the exclusive document which must be used by all state CSE agencies. An appropriately completed NMSN is considered to be a "Qualified Medical Child Support Order," and as such must be honored by the noncustodial parent's group health plan. This legislation also required the establishment of a Medical Support Working Group to make further recommendations to the Secretaries of Labor and Health and Human Services on how to improve medical support and to submit those recommendations to Congress.[6]

As evidenced in this brief history, since 1984, Congress has tried to increase provision of private health care coverage for children whose noncustodial parent has access to employer-based or group health insurance that is provided at a reasonable cost. This strategy was seen as a way to make noncustodial parents responsible for their children and lessen taxpayer burden by shifting the cost of providing health care to children from the taxpayers back to the noncustodial parents. For a detailed legislative history of provisions related to medical child support, see **Appendix A**.

In 2006, federal law defined the term "medical support" and required that states have procedures under which all child support orders that are enforced by CSE agencies must include a provision for medical support for the child to be provided by *either* or *both* parents. Federal law further stipulated that CSE agencies may enforce medical support against a custodial parent if health care coverage is available to the custodial parent at a reasonable cost.

Medical support adds complexity to the CSE program, in part, because the provision of medical child support can be imposed on either the noncustodial parent, the custodial parent, or both parents. Medical child support may be a significant additional expense for noncustodial parents.[7] In addition to the child support payment, noncustodial parents may be legally liable for paying health insurance premium costs, co-payments, deductibles, and/or unreimbursed medical expenses. High health insurance premiums may negatively impact how much disposable income the noncustodial parent has available to meet his or her financial child support order. If the premium is high, cash support may be substantially reduced, leaving the custodial parent without enough money to take care of the child's food, clothing, and shelter needs. Health care coverage of children and medical child support are not synonymous. A child could be covered by a custodial parent's health insurance plan and the child support order may not contain any provision for medical support from the noncustodial parent. Conversely, a child may be receiving cash medical support but not be insured.

Based on information from the federal Office of Child Support Enforcement (OCSE) in the Department of Health and Human Services (HHS), in the future, the establishment and enforcement of medical child support may become a CSE program performance measure, however, more needs to be done before that can occur. Thus, even though states submit medical support data, the information is not subject to an audit to determine if it is "complete and reliable." Also, because medical support establishment allows states to initiate legal medical support orders before determining whether or not the health insurance is affordable/reasonable,[8] state CSE agencies are severely hampered, if not totally stymied, in successfully enforcing medical child support orders. Data from OCSE indicate that there has been some improvement in the *establishment* of medical child support but considerably less improvement in the *enforcement* of medical child support. According to OCSE data, in FY2011, 81% of child support cases that had a child support order[9] included medical child support. In comparison, in FY1995, 61% of child support cases that had a child support order included medical child support. In contrast, the enforcement of medical support orders continues to be problematic. In FY2011, the medical support order was complied with in only 33% of the cases in which medical support had been ordered.[10] (See **Appendix B.)** The comparable figure in FY1995 was the same, 33%.

The CSE program has at its disposal a wide variety of methods by which to obtain child support obligations. Collection methods used by state CSE agencies include

- income withholding,
- intercept of federal and state income tax refunds,

- intercept of unemployment compensation,
- liens against property,
- reporting child support obligations to credit bureaus,
- intercept of lottery winnings,
- sending insurance settlement information to CSE agencies,
- authority to withhold or suspend driver's licenses, professional licenses, and recreational and sporting licenses of persons who owe past-due support,
- authority to seize assets of debtor parents held by public or private retirement funds and financial institutions, and
- authority for the Secretary of State to deny, revoke, or restrict passports of debtor parents.

Also included in their available methods to collect child support obligations, states use the threat of jail and actual incarceration.

Efforts to improve the establishment and enforcement of medical child support have a better chance of success if analyzed in the context of factors such as high health care costs, a decline in employer-provided health insurance coverage, an increase in the share of health insurance costs borne by employees, and a significant number of noncustodial parents who have low or moderate incomes. Moreover, it is important to recognize, as mentioned earlier, that cash support and medical support are not always compatible. For example, if premiums, co-payments, and deductibles for health insurance and medical care owed by noncustodial parents rise, equity might suggest that the cash child support payment of noncustodial parents be reduced to reflect their payment of these medical costs. Custodial parents may then have less income to provide for the basic food, clothing, and shelter needs of their children. Conversely, if medical child support is not available, the family would be more likely to be financially disadvantaged by routine health care needs of children and could face dire economic circumstances if a child becomes seriously ill.

However, it must be recognized that there is a lot of overlap between cash support and medical support. According to some CSE administrators, a primary reason for upward modifications of child support awards is care needed for a child with special needs. Many states combine any cash medical support payment to the custodial parent with the regular child support order as a single payment. Some states order that the parents will split all medical costs leaving it to the parents to work it out between themselves. Additionally some experts argue that routine medical expenses, including health insurance costs, are in fact rolled into the expenditures data used to calculate the cost of raising a child upon which child support guidelines are based.[11]

The public and policymakers generally agree that establishment and enforcement of medical support promotes equity in allocating childrearing costs between custodial and noncustodial parents, and usually saves federal and state dollars.[12]

In 2010, health reform legislation, P.L. 111-148 (the Patient Protection and Affordable Care Act; ACA), as amended by P.L. 111-152 (the Health Care and Education Reconciliation Act of 2010; HCERA) was enacted. The primary goal of the ACA is to increase access to health insurance for the millions of Americans without coverage.[13] The ACA expands federal private health insurance market requirements, and requires the creation of health insurance exchanges to provide individuals and small employers with access to insurance. It also expands Medicaid coverage at state option.[14] The ACA has at least one shared goal with the CSE program in that both are attempting to ensure that children have health care coverage.

CURRENT FEDERAL POLICY

Current federal law requires every child support order established by a state CSE agency to include a provision for medical child support.[15] States are required to include provisions for medical child support in their child support guidelines, and the CSE program is required to pursue private health care coverage when such coverage is available through a noncustodial parent's employer at a "reasonable" cost.[16]

A court or administrative agency may require an employee to provide health insurance for his/her children. They may also require an employee to purchase family coverage if child-only coverage is not available. Courts require coverage if it is available at a reasonable cost to an employee through the employer or other group health insurance (for example, a union). Employers are required to honor medical support orders established under state law. The cost of private health insurance or cash medical support is considered reasonable if the cost to the parent responsible for providing medical support does not exceed 5% of his or her gross income or, at state option, a reasonable alternative income-based numeric standard defined in state law, regulations, or court ruling. In applying the 5% or alternative state standard for the cost of private health insurance, the amount is the cost of adding the child(ren) to the existing coverage or the difference between self-only and family coverage.[17] For example, if a noncustodial parent is required to purchase family coverage in order to cover the requisite child(ren), the entire cost of the family coverage is not taken into account in calculating the 5% of the gross income amount.[18]

Federal law mandates that health insurance coverage for children be enforced, where appropriate, through the use of the National Medical Support Notice (NMSN).[19] To ensure that children receive health care coverage when it is available and required as part of a child support order, state CSE agencies send the NMSN to employers. The notice is designed to simplify the work of employers and plan administrators by providing uniform documents requesting information about health care coverage. States now are able to enforce such orders against both custodial and noncustodial parents. If health insurance is not available, states can pursue the joint sharing of expenses (i.e., cost-sharing)[20] associated with the child's medical care.

Providing for children's health care is a stated purpose of the CSE program. By connecting children to coverage through either of their parents' employers, Medicaid, CHIP, Health Insurance Exchanges (beginning in 2014),[21] or other options—the CSE program can assure that children will have continuous, stable access to health care as they grow up, and that the resources of both parents are being used most effectively for the child.[22]

To recap, medical child support can take several forms. States generally seek medical child support as sequenced below.

- The noncustodial or custodial parent may be ordered to provide health insurance if it is available at reasonable cost through the parent's employer.[23]
- The noncustodial parent may be ordered to pay for other private health insurance (health care coverage) premiums.
- The noncustodial parent may be ordered to reimburse the custodial parent for all or a portion of the costs of health insurance obtained by the custodial parent (on behalf of the child(ren)).
- If neither parent is able to obtain health insurance at a reasonable cost, the custodial parent may be ordered to apply on behalf of the child to a government- funded medical program such as Medicaid or the State Children's Health Insurance Program (CHIP). The cost of any Medicaid expenses or CHIP coverage (including premiums, co-pays, or coinsurance costs) may be added to the noncustodial parent's monthly child support payment.

- Both parents may be required to pay a percentage of "out-of-pocket" medical expenses that are not covered through insurance. The percentage is determined by the financial circumstances of each parent.
- If neither parent has private insurance and the children are not eligible for Medicaid or CHIP, the court may order the noncustodial parent to provide cash medical support in addition to the monthly child support payment; and/or the noncustodial parent may be ordered to pay additional amounts to cover a portion of ongoing medical bills or as reimbursement for uninsured medical costs.

When the noncustodial parent is ordered to pay cash medical support, generally it is included in the cash child support order and a single notice of income withholding is sent to the employer to withhold from the parent's paycheck. If the parent is ordered to provide insurance through the employer, the employer is required to enroll the child in health insurance coverage and withhold the necessary premium payments from the parent's income. The employer is required to send any amount withheld directly to the health care plan. In addition, employers must promptly notify the CSE agency whenever the noncustodial parent's, and, at state option, the custodial parent's employment is terminated. Conversely, state CSE agencies are required to promptly notify the employer when there is no longer a current medical support order in effect.[24]

Establishing and Enforcing Medical Child Support

Regulations on medical child support[25] require that child support guidelines[26] (at a minimum) address how the parents will provide for the child's or children's health care needs through health insurance coverage and/or through cash medical support. The guidelines cover whether the noncustodial parent, the custodial parent, or both parents will be required to carry health care insurance for the child or children, how uninsured health care expenses for children will be allocated between the parents, and whether there is a need for other types of medical support.[27]

Establishment

The CSE agency is required, on behalf of both welfare and non-welfare families, to pursue health care coverage when such coverage is available through a parent's employer.[28] The CSE agency must petition the court to include medical support in any order for child support when employment-related or other group health insurance is available to either parent at a reasonable cost.[29]

States have laws stipulating that insurers can no longer refuse to enroll a child in a health care plan because the parents are not married or because the child does not live in the same household as the enrolled parent. In addition, CSE agencies can require an employer to include a child on a medical insurance plan when the noncustodial parent participates in a group health plan but does not enroll the child.[30] Unless a custodial parent has satisfactory health insurance for the child or children other than Medicaid, the CSE agency can petition the court or administrative authority to include health insurance in a child support order when health insurance is, or may be, available to the noncustodial parent at reasonable cost.

If a custodial parent has access to better health insurance than the noncustodial parent or prefers to cover the child/children,[31] the child support order may increase the noncustodial parent's obligation to offset the cost. Court orders can also be modified to include medical child support.

The process of establishing medical child support is designed to determine, when neither parent has health insurance available to them at a reasonable cost, whether other coverage through the Medicaid or the State Children's Health Insurance Program (CHIP) is appropriate for the child. The guidelines process also is designed to consider whether the noncustodial parent has the resources to provide a set monetary amount ("cash medical support") towards a portion of the cost of health insurance provided by the custodial parent or coverage provided by the government.[32]

As mentioned earlier, federal law requires every child support order established by a state CSE agency to include a provision for medical child support (i.e., the child support order includes a medical support order/provision). Neither federal law nor regulations mandate the payment of medical costs as a stand-alone item. In some cases, medical support is imbedded in the general child support order. For example, an income shares[33] child support guidelines schedule usually incorporates some medical costs within the guideline schedule itself (e.g., $250 per year per child) and medical costs are considered as part of the basic child support obligation amount that is ordered to be paid by the obligated parent. Additionally, the costs of health insurance and/or medical costs not covered by insurance are apportioned between the parents based on the percentages of their respective shares of their combined net income.[34] In other cases, a provision requiring health insurance coverage and/or cash medical support could be included in the child support order.[35]

Enforcement

Although there is widespread agreement that many children still lack health care coverage, OCSE data indicate some improvement in the establishment and enforcement of medical child support. For example, in FY2011, 81% of child support cases with a child support order included medical child support and the medical support order was complied with in 33% of the cases. In that same fiscal year, medical support orders that stipulated the provision of health insurance coverage were applicable to 88% of all child support cases with a child support order, and were provided as ordered in 31% of those cases.[36] These data do not reflect children who might be covered by public programs such as Medicaid or CHIP. The option to include public coverage in the data reporting was not available to states until FY2012.[37]

As previously noted, in practice some medical child support orders are established before it has been determined that the employer-sponsored health coverage is affordable. Thus, one reason why coverage may not be provided as ordered (i.e., why enforcement rates of medical support are relatively low) may be because it is not available to the obligated parent at a reasonable rate. There is little that the CSE agency can do to enforce the existing medical support order in these circumstances.

New Hire Reporting

A major reform to the CSE program was established in the 1996 welfare reform law (P.L. 104- 193). It required states, by October 1, 1997, to establish an automated directory of new hires containing information from employers, including federal, state, and local governments and labor organizations, for each newly hired employee. The State Directory of New Hires (SDNH) must include the name, address and social security number of the employee and the employer's name, address, and tax identification number. This information is to be supplied by employers to the state's new hires directory within 20 days after the employee is hired. Within 3 business days after receipt of new hire information, the state directory of new hires is required to furnish the information to the National Directory of New Hires (NDNH).[38]

The NDNH is a database that contains personal and financial data on nearly every working American, as well as those receiving unemployment compensation.[39] The NDNH includes information from State Directories of

New Hires (SDNHs), State Workforce Agencies (SWAs), and federal agencies. The NDNH database does not include information about health insurance availability, cost, or quality.

The state CSE agency compares the information maintained in its SDNH with its database of noncustodial parents,[40] and also uploads the SDNH information to the NDNH, which contains new hire information reported by all states. Through automated computer interfaces, states regularly compare their databases of noncustodial parents responsible for paying child support or providing medical child support with the information available through the NDNH. Within two business days of identifying a new employer of a noncustodial parent through either the state or federal matching process, the state must send an income withholding order and/or a National Medical Support Notice (NMSN) to the employer.[41]

National Medical Support Notice (NMSN)

To help obtain health care coverage for children, Congress passed laws requiring states to send the NMSN to employers to enroll children in health care plans. Its purpose is to ensure that children receive health care coverage when it is available at a reasonable cost and required as part of a child support order. It is designed to simplify the employers' and plan administrators' workflow by providing uniform documents to obtain health care coverage for children.

Some states have chosen to centralize the National Medical Support Notice issuance process while other states allow local child support agencies to issue and provide follow-up on these notices.[42]

An appropriately completed NMSN is considered a "Qualified Medical Child Support Order (QMCSO),"[43] and as such must be honored by all health plans including federal agencies' group health plans. Pursuant to federal law, if a QMCSO names an employee who is not enrolled in the plan, but is eligible to enroll, the order is considered a legitimate/legal medical child support order.[44] As mentioned earlier in this report, establishing a medical child support order before it has been verified that the health plan is affordable can be problematic because CSE agencies have no authority to require a noncustodial parent to purchase health insurance that is not affordable and thereby these agencies are not in a position to enforce such an order.

The NMSN is usually mailed to the employer along with the income withholding notice. The NMSN contains two parts: (1) Part A - Notice to Withhold for Health Care Coverage and (2) Part B - Medical Support Notice to Plan Administrator.

When the employer receives a NMSN, the employer has two legally permissible options: (1) to inform the CSE agency that such coverage is not available, or (2) to notify the health insurance plan administrator to enroll the child or children. Once the health insurance plan administrator receives notification from the employer to enroll the children, the administrator has two options: (1) to provide an explanation to the CSE agency for non-enrollment; or (2) to enroll the child or children.[45]

If the employer provides health insurance to employees, the employer must forward Part B of the NMSN to the plan administrator. Once the employer is notified of enrollment, the employer must begin withholding for premiums. If employees have group health coverage through a union, the employer must forward the NMSN to the appropriate union representative. If the employer does not provide health insurance for employees, the employer must complete the Employer Response page of the NMSN and return it to the issuing CSE agency.

The CSE program has at its disposal a wide variety of methods by which to obtain child support obligations. The most effective child support enforcement tool is income withholding, a procedure by which automatic deductions are made from wages or other income. Once initiated, income withholding can keep child support flowing to the family on a regular basis. In FY2011, about 70% of the $31 billion ($22 billion) collected by the states for child support payments was obtained through income withholding, 5% (almost $2 billion) from the unemployment intercept offset, 7% ($2 billion) by way of the federal income tax refund offset, less than 1% ($209 million) from the state income tax refund offset, and 17% ($5 billion) from other sources.[46]

The states are not required to provide data on the results from sending employers the NMSN. However, the perception is that most NMSNs sent to employers do not result in a child being enrolled in an employer-sponsored health plan primarily because affordable family coverage is not offered. One study shows that issuing a NMSN to the noncustodial parent's employer results in 10-23% of children being enrolled in such a health plan.[47]

Medicaid Provisions Related to Child Support Enforcement

Medicaid Basics

The Medicaid program was enacted in 1965 as Title XIX of the Social Security Act (P.L. 89-97). Medicaid is a program funded by both the states and the federal government to provide health care coverage to low-income children, pregnant women, families with dependent children, the elderly, and individuals with disabilities. Although Medicaid is an entitlement program in federal budget terms, states choose whether to participate, and all 50 states, the District of Columbia and five territories (American Samoa, Guam, the Northern Mariana Islands, Puerto Rico, and the Virgin Islands) do so. If a state chooses to participate, it must follow federal rules in order to receive federal reimbursement that offsets at least 50% of its Medicaid costs.[48]

Federal rules require states with Medicaid programs to cover certain benefits (i.e., mandatory benefits). Certain other services may also be offered at state option. Most children eligible for Medicaid receive a comprehensive package of services including physician care; inpatient and outpatient hospitalization; laboratory testing and x-rays; and early and periodic screening, diagnostic and treatment (EPSDT) services. States must agree to pursue any third party who might be liable to pay medical bills of families enrolled in the Medicaid program.[49] If a family has access to private health care insurance (including that obtained through a child support order), that coverage is primary and Medicaid is secondary. The Medicaid program may pay other uncovered expenses.[50]

Among the groups of persons that are mandatorily covered are: poor families that meet the financial requirements (based on family size) of the former Aid to Families with Dependent Children (AFDC) program (as it was in effect in July 16, 1996);[51] pregnant women and children through age 6 with family income at or below 133% of the federal poverty level (FPL); and children ages 6 through 18 with family income at or below 100% FPL, rising to 133% FPL beginning in 2014 (or sooner at state option).[52]

States that choose to participate in the expansion of Medicaid under the ACA (beginning in 2014) will cover most adults under age 65 with incomes below 133% of the federal poverty level.

Assignment Provision

Pursuant to the Child Support Enforcement Amendments of 1984 (P.L. 98-369) custodial parents applying for or receiving Medicaid are required to assign to the state any medical support rights they or their children have,[53] including any rights to medical support arising out of a divorce decree or child support order.[54] "Assigning one's rights" to medical support to the state means that the custodial parent is giving the state the right to collect and retain any medical support that is owed to the custodial parent. Either an insurance company or an individual (such as the noncustodial parent) can be pursued by the state for payment of medical support.

Custodial parents who refuse to assign their child support rights to the state can be denied Medicaid coverage. If these parents are already receiving Medicaid benefits, their benefits can be terminated. However, the children are entitled to receive Medicaid benefits and those benefits cannot be terminated even if their parents refuse to assign to the state the children's medical support rights.[55]

In addition, Section 1902(a)(25)(H) of the Social Security Act requires states to have laws which automatically assign to the state a custodial parent's right to medical payments by third parties, to the extent that the Medicaid program has made a payment. This provision of law assigns to a state an individual's right to medical support whether or not an assignment has been put into effect and if the case is referred to the CSE agency, it is the CSE agency's responsibility to seek medical support for that child.

Cooperation Requirements

In addition, as a condition of eligibility for Medicaid coverage, custodial parents applying for or receiving Medicaid are required by Section 1912(a) of the Social Security Act to cooperate with the state in establishing the paternity of any eligible child born out of wedlock and in obtaining medical support and payment. Custodial parents applying for or receiving Medicaid must identify the noncustodial parent, be actively involved in establishing paternity (if that is an issue), participate in obtaining a medical support order, and assist in obtaining any benefits available under that order. As with assignment, if a custodial parent refuses to cooperate, her or his Medicaid benefits, but not the child's can be terminated.

The purpose behind the Medicaid assignment and cooperation requirements is to assist the state in pursuing any third party who may be legally liable for the payment of medical care and services on behalf of persons receiving Medicaid. Successful identification of any third party capable of providing or paying for medical care and services (1) releases the Medicaid program from paying for services that others should have been financing, (2) reduces medical costs to the states and the federal government provided under Medicaid, and (3) reinforces the concept of Medicaid as the payor of last resort. The term "third party" includes any individual, entity, or program that may be liable to pay all or part of the costs for medical care and services available under the Medicaid program. The term may also include any employment-related or other individual or group health insurance available to or through the child's parents.[56] In addition, it includes cash medical support payments from the noncustodial parent for Medicaid costs.

The CSE agency decides whether custodial parents are being cooperative in this process. The CSE agency makes an initial determination and periodically redetermines whether parents are "cooperating in good faith." The CSE agency notifies the parents and the Medicaid agency when such determinations are made. If the CSE agency decides that a custodial parent is not being cooperative, the notice will delineate the reasons for the finding. The Medicaid agency will then inform the parent that benefits are being denied or terminated for noncooperation with the CSE agency. The parent can request a hearing if he or she wishes to contest the finding. As discussed later, children remain eligible for Medicaid regardless of the parent's cooperation with the CSE program.

Medicaid Birthing Costs

The Medicaid program covers costs associated with the birth of a child for pregnant women whose income is below 133% of the federal poverty level or up to 185% of the federal poverty level at state option. The Medicaid-paid birth costs are an entitlement to the mother, and federal and state laws preclude recovery of these costs from the mother. However, in some states, paternity judgments and/or child support orders may require the repayment of birth costs that were paid by the state Medicaid program or by an individual, including the custodial parent, a grandparent, or another third party who paid the expenses for the pregnancy and the birth of the child. Some state statutes permit the state to recover these costs from a child's father if the parents are not married.[57]

The cost recovery effort is generally undertaken by CSE agencies. The CSE agencies generally retain a percentage of all recoveries, and the remainder is used to reimburse the Medicaid program.[58]

In the child support policy arena, there is concern that recovery of Medicaid birthing costs from low-income noncustodial fathers may increase the probability that such fathers will accumulate high child support arrearages which in some cases leads to reduced child support collections. Some observers assert that it may be ineffective to try to collect Medicaid birthing costs from fathers of children on Medicaid in many instances because many of those fathers themselves have low incomes and are unable to make the payments. They argue that such birthing costs inflate the amount of arrearages owed by noncustodial parents and often deter the noncustodial parent from paying any child support. When noncustodial parents perceive that the system is unfair or that the debt is too great to overcome, the likelihood that they will pay any child support decreases.[59]

More recently, some commentators have indicated that it is unproductive to require uninsured low-income noncustodial fathers, who may soon (pursuant to the ACA, as amended) be Medicaid-eligible themselves, to provide cash payments to the Medicaid program.

Exemptions from Medicaid CSE Rules

There are three exemptions from the Medicaid CSE rules: two good cause exemptions and the pregnancy exemption. Both the assignment and the cooperation requirement can be waived if a custodial parent can establish good cause for doing so. One way to establish good cause is to show that establishing paternity or pursuing medical support is against the best interests of the child. The other way is to show that establishing paternity or pursuing medical support is against the best interests of the individual or the person to whom Medicaid is being furnished because it is anticipated that cooperation will result in reprisal against, and cause physical or emotional harm to, that individual or another person.[60]

In 1990, Congress added another exception to the cooperation requirement. Pursuant to P.L. 101- 508 (the Omnibus Budget Reconciliation Act of 1990) poverty level pregnant women are not required to cooperate in establishing paternity or pursuing medical support from the child's father.[61] This exemption is only available during the pregnancy and for 60 days postpartum. After that, the mother must assign her medical support rights to the state and cooperate in establishing paternity and pursuing medical child support in order to continue her Medicaid coverage. According to one report: "*In creating this exception, Congress acknowledged studies that showed that it was both morally right and fiscally prudent to encourage as many pregnant women as possible to obtain pre-natal care. In the absence of such care, children suffer and public costs soar. ...It also recognized that the child support cooperation requirement was a potential barrier for the high-risk, low income women that would benefit most from it [pre-natal care].*"[62]

State Children's Health Insurance Program (CHIP)

In 1997, P.L. 105-33 (the Balanced Budget Act of 1997) established the State Children's Health Insurance Program (CHIP) under a new Title XXI of the Social Security Act.

Unlike the Medicaid program, CHIP is not an individual entitlement program. In 2009, P.L. 111-3 (the Children's Health Insurance Program

Reauthorization Act of 2009; CHIPRA) extended federal funding through FY2013. In 2010, the ACA, as amended, extended federal funding through FY2015.[63]

CHIP is a federal-state matching program that provides enhanced federal funds to states that offer health care coverage to uninsured children who are not eligible for Medicaid. CHIP builds on the Medicaid program by extending coverage to uninsured children whose family income is too high to qualify for Medicaid but who cannot afford private coverage. In order to encourage enrollment, many states use streamlined applications for CHIP and do not impose an assets test.[64]

States can offer CHIP coverage by expanding their Medicaid programs (financed with CHIP funds), creating separate CHIP programs, or devising a combination of both approaches. If a state expands its Medicaid program for CHIP purposes, then Medicaid rules (including the child support assignment and cooperation rules) apply. However, if the state sets up a separate CHIP program then the rules are somewhat different. There are no explicit child support assignment or cooperation provisions in CHIP. Whether they are Medicaid or CHIP eligible, children are to be covered regardless of whether or not their parents comply with CSE rules.[65] Even so, some commentators note that the administrative cost of enforcing cooperation rules, and the requirements placed on the custodial parent do in fact impact both programs.[66]

Health Insurance Exchanges

The ACA, as amended, requires health insurance exchanges to be established by January 1, 2014. Exchanges are new organizations that are intended to create a more organized and competitive marketplace for buying health insurance. Exchanges are to offer a choice of different health plans, certify plans that participate, and provide information to help consumers better understand their options. Essentially, exchanges are intended to bring together buyers and sellers of insurance, with the goal of increasing access to coverage. To make exchange coverage more affordable, certain individuals will receive premium assistance in the form of federal tax credits.[67]

Beginning in 2014, exchanges will serve primarily individuals buying insurance on their own and small businesses with up to 100 employees, though states can choose to include larger employers in the future. States are expected to establish exchanges—which can be a government agency or a nonprofit organization—with the federal government stepping in if a state does not set one up. States can create multiple exchanges, so long as only one serves each geographic area, and can work together to form regional exchanges. The federal government will offer technical assistance to help states set up exchanges.[68] Exchanges will also screen individuals for eligibility for certain public insurance programs (e.g., Medicaid) and connect them with appropriate agencies.

For individuals seeking health coverage, exchanges will offer qualified health plans for purchase, and help certain individuals obtain federally subsidized premium and cost-sharing assistance[69] to assist low to middle income individuals. To qualify for subsidies in the exchanges, individuals, among other things, may not have access to employer-sponsored health insurance that is considered affordable. The ACA considers employer coverage "unaffordable" if the employee's contribution toward the employer's lowest-cost self-only premium exceeds 9.5% of household income.

Given that the premium assistance will be provided in the form of tax credits, they will be administered through individual income tax returns (although advance payments will go directly to insurers). The tax credits can only be obtained by qualifying individuals who file federal income tax returns. Moreover, with the new tax-based definition of family size (pursuant to the ACA), a child claimed as a dependent on a custodial parent's tax return will not be counted in determining the family size of the noncustodial parent's household. The ACA states that in such cases, an exchange premium tax credit would not be allowed for the noncustodial parent with respect to the child.[70] This means that although such a child could receive coverage as part of the noncustodial parent's coverage, the noncustodial parent would not be eligible for the premium tax credit to offset some of the cost of that coverage.[71] Since only one parent can claim the child as a dependent, this may result in different choices about which parent claims the child for tax purposes. In other words, noncustodial parents would only be allowed to benefit from the exchange premium tax credit on behalf of their nonresident child(ren) if, and only if, the noncustodial parent could legitimately claim the child(ren) as a dependent on his or her federal income tax return.[72]

Collaboration among CSE, Medicaid, and CHIP Agencies (and the Exchanges)

Many analysts agree that one way to increase the establishment and enforcement of medical child support is to encourage the coordination of activities of the state Medicaid and CSE agencies. The state CSE agency and the state Medicaid agency could be mandated to work out automatic referrals between the two programs to assure that children in the Medicaid program have access to CSE services and that children in the CSE program have access to health care coverage options.[73]

The medical child support assignment and cooperation requirements link low-income families with the CSE program, automatically enabling them to obtain CSE services at no cost.[74] Moreover, if the CSE program can use the assignment to obtain private health care coverage for a child through a noncustodial parent's private health insurance, there are potential savings to the Medicaid program.[75]

Some custodial parents do not comply with the medical child support assignment and cooperation requirements because of fear of domestic violence if they pursue support. Others don't have a clear understanding of what they are supposed to do or have a hard time doing what they are supposed to do in order to comply. Still others may be inappropriately denied an exemption from the requirements. The penalty for noncompliance with the Medicaid rules for the custodial parent is denial of Medicaid coverage for that parent.[76] Many analysts contend that the medical child support assignment and cooperation requirements, originally mandated in 1984, are no longer necessary. They argue that most low-income families with noncustodial parents are fully aware of the CSE program and its benefits and are already program participants, thus there is no need to try to coerce them into the CSE program. Some analysts assert that instead of helping families acquire medical care, the Medicaid assignment and cooperation requirements often add unnecessary confusion and/or increase the complexity of a complicated program. Other observers argue that the underlying assumption of medical child support—namely that substantial numbers of noncustodial parents have access to employer-based health insurance which if pursued and obtained would significantly reduce Medicaid costs—is flawed, resulting in unnecessary barriers to eligible custodial parents enrolling in the Medicaid program.[77]

As mentioned earlier, children remain eligible for Medicaid regardless of the parent's cooperation with the CSE program. Children who are not eligible for Medicaid (i.e., family income too high) may be eligible to participate in CHIP. In contrast to Medicaid, this program does not contain a child support cooperation requirement.

Administratively, it is difficult to streamline the Medicaid and CHIP application process given that Medicaid rules require states to obtain child support information and CHIP rules do not.[78] Different forms and procedures for the two programs that stem from the medical child support requirements generally lengthen the Medicaid application process, require additional paperwork and verification of certain information (with actual social security cards and birth certificates), and possible in-person interviews if the parent is trying to make a case for a good cause exemption. The ACA's coverage provisions to a certain extent overshadow CSE/Medicaid/CHIP application reporting requirements. P.L. 111-148 (ACA) requires simplification of the application/enrollment process. Beginning in 2014, income eligibility for most Medicaid eligible groups will be based on Modified Adjusted Gross Income (MAGI). With the switch to MAGI, states will no longer rely on disregards and deductions in determining whether someone qualifies for benefits for most Medicaid eligibility groups. Instead, there will be a single methodology that will determine how income is counted.[79] The use of MAGI is intended to standardize and simplify income eligibility across states and between Medicaid, CHIP and the exchange premium subsidies, and help lower state administrative costs related to eligibility determinations, by adopting what is essentially a gross income test.[80] The ACA also requires coordination with state Health Insurance Exchanges.

The ACA's coverage provisions related to the expansion of Medicaid eligibility and establishment of health insurance exchanges were designed to be mutually exclusive. For example, the ACA requires exchanges to identify individuals eligible for Medicaid, CHIP, and premium credits. Likewise, Medicaid and CHIP programs must be able to determine an applicant's eligibility for subsidized exchange coverage. These eligibility determination and enrollment provisions are intended to ensure that there is coordination between the exchanges, Medicaid, and CHIP, and to ensure that individuals are enrolled in a plan that offers benefits and cost-sharing protections suited to their family income.[81] How this collaboration will work when both noncustodial and custodial parents are eligible is unclear.

Medicaid Eligibility Final Regulation (MEFR) Section 435.940 and Section 435.945 require states to administer their programs in the best interest of applicants and beneficiaries and establish an eligibility verification plan. MEFR Section 435.1200 provides that in determining eligibility, state Medicaid and CHIP agencies will have the option to either make the final Medicaid and CHIP eligibility determination based on the exchange's initial review or accept a final eligibility determination made by an exchange that uses state eligibility rules and standards. The regulation goes on to clarify the standards and guidelines to ensure a simple, coordinated, accurate, and timely eligibility determination process regardless of the option elected by the state.

MEFR Section 435.912 provides that in cases where the Medicaid agency is evaluating an individual's eligibility for another insurance affordability program, the agency must transfer the information promptly and without need for further information or verification, and requires that the Medicaid agency make a website available to provide program information and to facilitate enrollment in insurance affordability programs. MEFR Section 457.343 provides for a data-driven CHIP eligibility review using information already available to the agency in the electronic account or from other reliable data sources. This section of MEFR provides that individuals determined ineligible for CHIP will be assessed for eligibility for other insurance affordability programs and provides for electronic transfer of account information and the timely reporting of and action on changes in an individual's circumstances.[82]

Beginning in 2014, the health insurance exchanges will be part of the health care arena. According to HHS, exchanges will be best able to perform verification of access to employer- sponsored coverage on a real-time basis during the enrollment process if they can access one or more authoritative data sources that capture the relevant information in an automated fashion. However, data sources that contain all the information exchanges will be seeking to verify do not currently exist. Until more comprehensive data sources are available, an interim strategy for verifying employer-sponsored coverage is needed to meet the following goals: (1) ensuring access to affordable coverage for consumers, (2) minimizing burdens on exchanges, individuals and employers, and (3) supporting eligibility determinations to ensure accuracy in the administration of advance payments of the premium tax credit. The interim strategy that HHS has proposed would allow an individual requesting an eligibility determination for advance payments of the exchange premium tax credit to attest to whether he or she has access to affordable employer-sponsored coverage that meets minimum value standards, and whether he or she reasonably expects to be enrolled in such coverage during the months in which he or she plans to seek coverage through the exchange. An exchange would then verify this information. HHS is considering proposing that the exchange compare the individual's attestation to existing data sources and records that could potentially be available to the exchange such as the National Directory of New Hires or unemployment databases. HHS anticipates using this interim approach for two years while additional data sources become available.[83]

Some commentators note that the state-based nature of exchanges may result in many challenges for the CSE program given that about a third of CSE cases are interstate cases.

POTENTIAL IMPACT OF THE ACA ON THE CSE PROGRAM

For more than 20 years, from 1984 through 2005, many in Congress held the view that noncustodial parents with affordable private health insurance should be made to include their children in such coverage. This was seen as the way to make noncustodial parents responsible for the health care needs of their children and lessen taxpayer burden by shifting costs from the taxpayers back to the noncustodial parents.

Before 2006, the medical child support requirement was based on the assumption that most children enrolled in public health coverage could obtain private coverage through the noncustodial parent. However, the ability of a noncustodial parent to provide private health coverage to his or her children is largely a function of income. In most cases, low-income noncustodial parents do not have access to employer-sponsored health insurance, and never did, and when such insurance is available, it is often not affordable or actual coverage by the provider is inaccessible or impractical because the noncustodial parent's employer-sponsored coverage relies on a local network of health care providers that are too far from his or her children.[84]

Pursuant to P.L. 111-148 (ACA, as amended), beginning in 2014 larger employers (i.e., certain employers with at least 50 full-time equivalent employees) will be required to either offer health insurance or be subject to a penalty if one of their full-time workers receives a subsidy to buy coverage through an exchange.[85] It is not yet known whether these aspects of the ACA will increase the number of employers who will offer private health insurance to their employees.

Also, pursuant to the ACA (as amended), certain individuals will have guaranteed access to health coverage outside the employment setting. It is expected that many employers will still decline to offer health insurance, and workers in those firms (and others) will either purchase insurance through the new exchanges or enroll themselves and their families in Medicaid if they are eligible or enroll their children in CHIP. In addition to small employers, beginning in 2014, the exchanges will provide new opportunities for individuals to access private health insurance, and provide access to premium tax credits and cost-sharing subsidies offered through the exchanges to make coverage in the private health insurance market more affordable for families no longer eligible for Medicaid.[86]

Under the ACA, as amended, beginning in 2014, individuals with household income between 100% and 400% of the federal poverty level will be able to obtain federally subsidized health insurance coverage through the health insurance exchanges.[87] In addition, the ACA currently prohibits coverage exclusions for preexisting health conditions in children under age 19 and effective January 1, 2014, the ACA will prohibit coverage exclusions for preexisting health conditions for all individuals regardless of age. Moreover, currently, health plans that provide dependent coverage must extend that existing coverage to children under age 26.[88]

The ACA adds more complexity to the CSE program but also may lead to health care coverage for more U.S. children.[89] Most analysts maintain that existing medical child support policies must be updated and/or revised to align with ACA reforms (and anticipated reforms) to children's health care coverage. There are many unanswered questions and many concerns. The four questions raised below highlight some issues about how the ACA will interact with the CSE program. Although the discussion below does not answer the questions per se, it provides background and context to the four concerns.

Will the Eligibility-Enrollment Gap in Federally Funded Health Care Be Eliminated?

In 2011, 9.4% of the 74.1 million children under age 18 in the U.S. did not have health insurance (7 million children).[90] Children in poverty are more likely to be uninsured than all children. This is somewhat surprising given that the Medicaid and CHIP programs were established to provide health care to low-income children and adults. In 2011, 13.8% of children in poverty did not have health insurance.[91] Earlier data (2008) shows that 11% of child support-eligible children did not have any source of health insurance.[92] It appears that the child support-eligible population and the child poverty population overlap. According to earlier data found in a 2011 HHS report, 44% of the estimated 26 million child support-eligible children[93] lived in low-income families with incomes less than 100% of the federal poverty level, 24% lived in families with incomes between 100% and 199% of the federal poverty level, an additional 21% lived in families with incomes between 200% and 399% of the federal poverty level, and 11% lived in families with incomes above 400% of the federal poverty level (based on 2008 data).[94]

The 2011 HHS report indicated that the majority of child support-eligible children qualify for public health care coverage through their state Medicaid or CHIP programs, but that many of them are not enrolled. Expanded efforts to enroll eligible children could have a major impact on reducing the number of uninsured in the child support population and in reducing the rate of uninsurance among children.[95] P.L. 111-3 (CHIPRA) included a five-year performance bonus payment program to states (that started in 2009) to encourage states to find and enroll eligible children in CHIP, in an effort to make enrollment and retention easier for eligible children and their families.[96]

In addition, a number of provisions in the ACA (as amended) require states to design and operate coordinated, technology-supported enrollment processes to assist individuals who lack access to affordable employer-based coverage in obtaining health coverage through Medicaid, CHIP, or the exchange. The law requires states to develop consumer-friendly application processes for these public health subsidy programs, coordinate across them to enable seamless transitions, and reduce the burdens of application and renewal by minimizing the up-front information and documentation required to establish eligibility and instead developing procedures that tap available data from other sources.[97] (These provisions are sometimes referred to as the screen and enroll requirements.)

There is general agreement that the CSE agency should work more closely with Medicaid/CHIP to ensure that children who have access to private health care coverage obtain such coverage, and that those who are only eligible for publicly-subsidized health coverage are actually enrolled in the Medicaid or CHIP programs. In conjunction with P.L. 111-3 (CHIPRA), HHS Secretary Kathleen Sebelius has stressed the importance of ongoing outreach efforts and simplification strategies through the *Connecting Kids to Coverage Challenge*, calling upon leaders at all levels of government and the private sector to find and enroll all uninsured children who are eligible for Medicaid and CHIP, and keep them covered for as long as they qualify.[98] In keeping with this initiative, state CSE programs were given the flexibility to improve the coordination between the CSE program, Medicaid, and CHIP to be consistent with P.L. 111-3 and the Secretary's goal of enrolling all eligible uninsured children in Medicaid and CHIP by 2014.[99]

Will Concerns Related to Affordability and Adequacy of Health Care Be Resolved?

In the child welfare arena, it is urged that health care coverage be available, accessible, affordable, and stable. However, requiring and enforcing health insurance may negatively affect the custodial parent and child as well as the noncustodial parent.

As explained earlier, state medical child support laws and the NMSN process are designed to ensure enrollment of a child in an appropriate health care plan, if health care coverage is available at "reasonable cost" to the noncustodial parent or the custodial parent through his or her employer.

With respect to the CSE program, health care coverage is considered "reasonable" if the cost does not exceed 5% of the noncustodial or custodial parent's gross income[100] (or another reasonable alternative income-based numeric standard provided by the state).[101] As mentioned earlier, federal regulations have defined reasonable cost so that it is not based on the actual cost the parent pays for health insurance coverage, but rather on the marginal cost of covering the child or children in question. Federal law, under the Consumer Credit Protection Act (CCPA), stipulates that income withholding for child support purposes must not exceed 65% of the disposable earnings of a parent who owes child support.[102]

The average annual health insurance premium contribution of workers for 2012 was estimated to be $4,316 for family plan coverage.[103] According to a recent report that summarized 2012 health care benefits of nonfederal private and public employers: For family coverage,

- 6% of covered workers are in plans that require no contribution for family coverage,
- 43% of covered workers are in plans that require them to make a contribution of less than or equal to a quarter of the total premium,[104]
- 37% are in plans that require them to pay more than a quarter but no more than half of the premium, and
- 14% are in plans that require more than half of the premium.

According to another study, in 2008, 24% of child support-eligible children[105] were living in families with income under the federal poverty level, 44% lived in families with income between 100% and 199% of the federal poverty level, 21% were in families with income between 200% and 399% of poverty, and 11% were in families with income of 400% of the federal poverty level or more.[106] The federal poverty level for a family of 3 was $17,600 in 2008.[107] Based on 2008 data, a health plan contribution of $880[108] or more generally would be considered above "reasonable cost" (5% of gross income) for a mother with two children living in any state other than Alaska or Hawaii.[109]

In recent years, health insurance premiums have increased and fewer employers offer health care benefits. Some observers contend that these are some of the factors that have diminished the value of the 5% standard. There are some data that indicate that the 5% threshold is too low and that in many, if not most, instances such a threshold would result in relatively few cases of employer-provided health insurance being considered reasonable.[110]

The final regulations regarding medical child support stipulate that in applying the 5% threshold or alternative state standard for the cost of private health insurance, the cost is the cost of adding the child or children to the existing coverage or the difference between self-only and family coverage. HHS agreed with commenters in the preamble to the final rule who responded to the proposed rule by stating that the full cost of a family health care insurance plan probably would exceed the reasonable cost standard thereby making it considerably less likely that the designated parent would be required to provide coverage through private health insurance.[111]

Some observers contend that low-income noncustodial parents should never have to pay more than 5% of their gross income on health coverage. They recommend that once premiums, deductible, and cost sharing exceed 5% of the noncustodial parent's gross income, all charges should stop for the year.[112]

Most states operate under the premise that if the custodial parent provides the health care coverage, the noncustodial parent's basic child support payment is supposed to increase, to reflect some contribution from the noncustodial parent toward the cost. Conversely, if the noncustodial parent provides the coverage, the cash support award is supposed to decrease, to reflect the fact that the noncustodial parent is subsidizing the cost of health care coverage through a separate deduction from wages toward the premium. The results may be problematic. If the premium associated with the health care coverage is too high, the result may be that the basic child support payment would be substantially reduced, leaving the custodial parent without enough money to take care of the child's or children's food, clothing, and shelter needs. If a child support order is not appropriately adjusted downward, the noncustodial parent is less likely to be able to comply with his or her child support order and this could lead to the accumulation of unmanageable arrearages.

The Medicaid program currently covers pregnant women and children through age 6 with family income at or below 133% of the federal poverty level (FPL) and children ages 6 through 18 with family income at or below 100% FPL, rising to 133% FPL beginning in 2014 (or sooner at state option). Moreover, under the ACA, as amended, (beginning in 2014) states will have the option to expand Medicaid coverage to include nearly all adults under age

65 with modified adjusted gross income (MAGI) at or below 133% of the FPL. Given that the majority of uninsured children are currently already eligible for Medicaid or CHIP, the Medicaid expansions are expected to have more impact on their parents or childless adults. Even so, some research indicates that when parents are insured so too are their children.[113]

As noted earlier, beginning in 2014, individuals who do not have access to affordable employer- sponsored insurance or other minimum essential coverage may be eligible to receive advanced premium tax credits for private insurance that they purchase through the health insurance exchange.[114] According to a CRS report:

> While there is no widely accepted definition of individual "affordability" when it comes to health insurance premiums, and other health-care related out-of-pocket costs, ACA sets insurance premium credits for persons, and their covered dependents, such that individuals and families will be required to spend no more than a specified percentage of income on premiums for specified health insurance plans in an exchange. Insurance premium credits under ACA will extend to individuals and families with modified adjusted gross income (hereinafter referred to simply as "income" with respect to ACA) between 100% and 400% FPL. ACA will provide premium credit support scaled to individual and family income relative to poverty such that eligible families' and individuals' premium contributions will be limited from 2.0% to 9.5% of income. Individuals and families with income at or above 400% of poverty will be ineligible for premium credits.[115]

As indicated earlier, only one parent can claim the child as a dependent on his or her federal income tax return, and the policies under the ACA may result in different choices about which parent claims the child for tax purposes. Noncustodial parents would be able to benefit from the exchange premium tax credit on behalf of their nonresident child(ren) if, and only if, the noncustodial parent could legitimately claim the child(ren) as a dependent on his or her federal income tax return.

Although private health care coverage has some advantages over public coverage—namely greater likelihood of full family coverage, a wider range of providers, no stigma, less taxpayer burden, and greater satisfaction with various aspects of care[116]—there are some instances when Medicaid or CHIP is preferred over private coverage. For example, public coverage often results in lower out-of-pocket costs, and for children, especially those with chronic or long-term disabilities, Early and Periodic Screening, Diagnostic, and

Treatment (EPSDT) benefits are unlimited (based on medical necessity, if access is not an issue).

Does Mandatory Health Care Coverage Negate the Need for Medical Child Support?

Securing medical coverage for children is a stand-alone goal and not merely a subset of other CSE goals. According to OCSE documents, the medical support goal is operationalized by establishing child support orders with a medical support component and by actually securing health coverage for children.[117]

As mentioned earlier, health care coverage of children and medical child support are not synonymous. A child could be covered by a custodial parent's health insurance plan but the noncustodial parent may not be sharing in the paying of premiums, co-payments, or other costs associated with the child's medical care. Conversely, a child may be receiving cash medical support but not be insured. When the ACA is fully implemented, access to affordable health care coverage may be less of an issue. If that is the case, policymakers might consider eliminating the establishment of health care coverage as a component of medical child support. Medical child support could thereby be defined as the noncustodial parent's payment of deductibles, co- payments, and other costs associated with a child's medical care and expenses. Whether or not this should require a separate medical support order or just be another component of the child support would need to be considered.

The federal government provides 66% of the funding for CSE program activities,[118] including those related to medical support. In order to receive any federal funding, states and/or local governments must provide 34% of the funds needed to operate their CSE programs. In the past, when Congress wanted to encourage activity in an area it considered vital to the effectiveness of the CSE program, it offered federal financial participation (FFP) at a higher level.[119] The 2003 report of the Medical Child Support Working Group[120] recommended that Congress provide enhanced FFP at a 90% rate for medical child support activities to encourage states to more aggressively pursue medical support enforcement.

In addition to the 66% federal matching rate, the federal government provides to states an incentive payment to encourage them to operate effective CSE programs. A state's incentive payment is based on its success in meeting certain performance criteria.[121] P.L. 105-200 (enacted in 1998) established the revised CSE incentive payment system and also required the HHS Secretary, in consultation with state CSE directors and representatives of children potentially eligible for medical support, to develop a medical support incentive measure based on the state's effectiveness in establishing and enforcing medical child support obligations. The medical support incentive was to be part of the performance-based child support incentive system.[122] The 1998 law required that a report on this new incentive measure be submitted to Congress not later than October 1, 1999. Although a report was submitted (in March 1999), it recommended that the use of a medical support performance measure be postponed due to data limitations.[123]

To date, the CSE program has never had an incentive performance measure for medical child support. Although medical support data is now collected by the states, that information is not currently used to compute incentive payments[124] or penalties and, according to OCSE, there are no immediate plans to use it in connection with the incentive payment system. A medical support incentive measure has been put on hold so as to determine what policy is appropriate given the ACA.[125] Medical support data currently provided by states are not required to be determined complete and reliable based on an audit by OCSE.

It should also be noted that although incentive payments are additional income for state CSE programs, in that they are required to be reinvested into the CSE program (or a related activity), they are no longer matched with federal dollars.[126] Thus, their impact on the CSE program has been significantly lessened.[127]

Some observers maintain that the CSE program is very complex and that success in terms of increased child support collections is not merely based on the proper functioning of the program but also on the economy and whether noncustodial parents are employed. They note that child support payments collected by CSE agencies increased from $1 billion in FY1978 to $27.3 billion in FY2011, and that the number of children whose paternity was established or acknowledged increased from 111,000 in FY1978 to 1.687 million in FY2011. But they further point out that regardless of some success, the CSE program still collects only 20% of child support obligations for which it has responsibility if arrearage payments are taken into account (otherwise, 62%)[128] and collects payments for only 57% of its caseload.[129] They contend that it should be expected that enforcement of medical child support by identifying and enrolling children in health insurance plans would be at least as hard as the enforcement of cash child support. Also, with the federal government no longer matching state incentive payments, the CSE program during this time of added complexity and many unknowns is likely to have less revenue at its disposal.

The underlying question remains unanswered—given that the ACA mandates health insurance coverage beginning in 2014, should the CSE program be revised and restructured so that the responsibility of establishing health insurance coverage is no longer under its bailiwick? There is no easy answer. Some commentators who support narrowing the focus of the CSE program with regard to medical child support maintain that the CSE program is well positioned and has strong tools to collect cash support, so focusing on cash support (including cash medical support) would be an efficient and effective role for the CSE program given the enactment of the ACA.[130] Others contend that medical support including health care coverage is an integral part of the CSE program and should remain so.[131]

Does the ACA Create an Overlap of CSE and IRS Duties and Responsibilities?

Among the new responsibilities of the Internal Revenue Service (IRS) in connection with the ACA is administering the mandate for individuals to purchase health coverage or be subject to a penalty on their individual federal income tax returns.

Pursuant to P.L. 111-148 (ACA), both custodial and noncustodial parents may become eligible for Medicaid coverage, or one or both parents may qualify for subsidies to purchase coverage in the health insurance exchange (beginning in 2014). However, the parent who claims the child as a dependent for tax purposes (generally the custodial parent) will be legally responsible for complying with the requirement to obtain health insurance coverage for the child. Such parents also will be eligible for any subsidies (i.e., the exchange premium tax credit) on behalf of her or his child as well as be subject to any penalties resulting from noncompliance with the health insurance mandate.

Some commentators contend that it is inequitable and unfair to subject custodial parents to penalties for noncompliance with ACA health insurance mandates especially if the relevant noncustodial parent is not required to pay his or her appropriate share of the costs associated with their child's medical care (i.e., co-payments, deductibles, and other expenses). They note that under federal regulations, states have the option not to enforce medical support orders ascribed to custodial parents. Others note that custodial parents can agree in writing to allow the noncustodial parent to claim the child as a dependent and thereby use the exchange. The noncustodial parent would thus benefit from the exchange premium credit and be held accountable to ACA compliance requirements as well. However, they point out that noncustodial parents living in different states from their children would not be permitted to enroll such child(ren) in a state that is not the home state of the child(ren). Given that about one-third of CSE cases are interstate cases, this exception is notable. Some observers indicate that there probably will be a need for a lot of coordination between the exchanges and the CSE program and perhaps revised CSE and/or exchange regulations.[132]

Beginning in 2014, taxpayers will have to start providing proof on their federal income tax returns that they have health insurance. Those who do not get qualified health insurance will be required to pay the penalty or tax starting in the 2014 tax year, unless they are exempt because of low income or religious beliefs, or because they are a member of an American Indian tribe.[133] P.L. 111-148 (ACA) allows the IRS to withhold federal income tax refunds to collect the penalty. As mentioned earlier, the CSE program also has a program under which past-due child support is withheld from federal income tax refunds. The result may be increased competition for the limited resources of noncustodial parents between the IRS and the CSE program.

The CSE program is required by federal law to enforce medical child support. If in the case in question, medical child support includes health insurance coverage[134] then the duties of both the CSE and IRS agencies will overlap because in that case they are both required under existing federal law to ensure that health insurance is actually provided. Program administrators generally agree that it is inefficient to duplicate another program's functions and duties.

CONCLUSION

During the debate on the original CSE legislation that was enacted in 1975, its chief sponsor, Senator Russell Long, who at the time was the chairman of the Senate Finance Committee, stated:

> Should our welfare system be made to support the children whose father cavalierly abandons them—or chooses not to marry the mother in the first place? Is it fair to ask the American taxpayer—who works hard to support his own family and to carry his own burden—to carry the burden of the deserting father as well? Perhaps we cannot stop the father

> from abandoning his children, but we can certainly improve the system by obtaining child support from him and thereby place the burden of caring for his children on his own shoulders where it belongs.[135]

Back in the early days of the CSE program, families receiving Aid to Families with Dependent Children (AFDC) benefits comprised about 85% (FY1978 data) of the CSE caseload.[136] AFDC families were automatically eligible for and entitled to Medicaid benefits. In fact, during that period the primary goals of the CSE program were (1) to reduce public expenditures on the AFDC (and Medicaid) program by obtaining child support from noncustodial parents on a consistent and ongoing basis and (2) to help some families to remain self-sufficient and off public assistance by providing the requisite CSE services.

Just as the CSE program expanded/revised its mission over the years from welfare cost-recovery to service delivery, the CSE program, pursuant to the Deficit Reduction Act of 2005 (P.L. 109- 171; enacted in February 2006) expanded its view of who should be responsible for obtaining health care for children. The CSE agency no longer focuses exclusively on the noncustodial parent, but rather considers a wider range of options. The CSE agency now examines the ability of either or both parents to secure and/or provide medical support. Medical support is generally provided in the form of private health care coverage, but it also can be in the form of cash payments. If private health insurance is not available to either parent, Medicaid and/or CHIP benefits are sought and either the noncustodial parent or custodial parent or both are responsible for paying any applicable co-pays and deductibles.

As noted earlier, most Americans view health care for their children and for themselves as one of their top concerns. There is evidence that health care coverage improves prenatal care (thereby reducing infant mortality and low birth weight); reduces avoidable hospitalizations of children; and increases the probability that children will receive recommended immunizations. It is generally agreed that access to and provision of health care improves outcomes for children.[137]

One of the goals President Obama set for health reform is provision of quality, affordable coverage to those who don't have health insurance.[138] By connecting children to the right coverage for them—coverage through either of their parents' employers, Medicaid, CHIP, exchanges, or other options—the CSE program can help assure that children will have continuous, stable access to health care as they grow up, and that the resources of both parents are being used most effectively for the child.[139]

There is general agreement that new methods need to be devised to help families who say that they do not know whether their child is eligible for publicly funded health care, do not know how to apply, or find the application processes too difficult. Some experts note that sharing data among programs can cut administrative costs, strengthen programs, and help more families access the benefits for which they are eligible.[140]

Because CSE data and information are often stored in disconnected systems across a multitude of data centers and because data elements are defined differently by various organizations, programs, and entities, it is often hard to exchange data and correctly understand its meaning. According to the OCSE Commissioner:

> Technology has the power to help break down silos between state health and human services programs and improve customer service. The promise of interoperable computer systems is that families will not have to go through multiple applications, interviews, and appointments to receive services and taxpayers will save money.[141]

According to testimony related to data standards and electronic information exchange in the CSE program:

> Sound standards establish a technological vocabulary that allows parties with various perspectives to speak the same language when discussing electronic information and data exchanges. Further, the existence of quality standards provides a level playing field for the vendors that provide software and services to the governmental entities using them. ... As the quantity and complexity of the systems we operate increases, standards can help to insure that a common vocabulary exists for all of us to use in facilitating good and efficient government.[142]

The OCSE Commissioner also has stated that data exchange standardization requirements "*will eventually establish a common set of data elements and definitions in a format easily exchanged between different human services systems, and in fact with any system.*"[143] The Commissioner further stated: "*With interoperable systems, we may do a better job of serving the whole person and the whole family; we may more effectively share services, streamline information and business systems, and minimize duplicative costs to build, maintain and update redundant computer systems.*"[144] Moreover, according to the Commissioner:

> The Affordable Care Act (ACA) is spurring states across the Nation to create new eligibility and enrollment computer systems for Medicaid and health insurance exchanges. The ACA presents a unique opportunity for state health and human services programs to integrate their systems both vertically and horizontally, and bring our programs one step closer to the "no wrong door" approach to service delivery. In the past, this was not possible due to the requirement to cost allocate federal dollars across multiple programs. However, through December 31, 2015, states can design, develop and implement system modules that perform common functions across all health and human services programs with enhanced 90/10 federal funding if they request a federal cost allocation waiver. The technology is here to begin to integrate health and human services systems. Linking them will accomplish two goals: improve client outcomes and enhance operational efficiency.[145]

The purpose behind this approach is to develop a standard format so as to improve the ability of two or more systems or entities to exchange information and to correctly use the information that has been exchanged. It is asserted that this approach together with streamlined applications, automatic enrollment, telephone interviews, e-signatures, and other efforts to share data across programs help individuals and families get the assistance and support they need quickly without the need for redundant eligibility screenings, applications, or data verification. Proponents of these methods contend that by reducing steps in the eligibility determination and recertification processes, efficiencies and administrative savings can be obtained.[146]

As mentioned earlier, the ACA (as amended) requires states to implement an electronic look up of eligibility information that the state may have on file from some other sources (e.g., income, citizenship status, family composition, information on file from another social welfare program such as TANF or SNAP, etc.). With the transition to MAGI (modified adjusted gross income) and this new beneficiary-focused system, individuals will only be required to supply eligibility information that does not match that which is on record with the state, or information that is missing from the shared eligibility system.

Beginning January 1, 2014, the ACA is expected to expand health insurance coverage to millions of individuals through new health insurance exchanges and expansions in Medicaid. However, questions remain regarding how the ACA will impact medical child support. Some observers contend that with its history of developing new strategies for collection of child support payments and better customer service, the CSE program will successfully handle future challenges. They suggest that the CSE program may have to redefine medical support, or pursue medical support only in cases in which children receive health care from public programs such as Medicaid or CHIP, or allow the Internal Revenue Service to take over the enforcement of medical support. Others note that the CSE program is already having a hard time successfully serving custodial parents. They suggest that the CSE program re-emphasize the need to include medical expenses in the child support order and perhaps expend any resources gained from eliminating its role in the enforcement of medical support on helping low-income noncustodial parents obtain employment so they can fulfill their child support obligations.

APPENDIX A. LEGISLATIVE HISTORY OF MEDICAL CHILD SUPPORT PROVISIONS

Just as Temporary Assistance for Needy Families (TANF) recipients must assign their child support rights to the state, so too must Medicaid recipients assign their medical support rights to the state. The impetus for the federal government moving into the arena of financial child support was to reduce federal expenditures on the former Aid to Families with Dependent Children (AFDC) entitlement program (replaced in 1996 by the time-limited TANF block grant program). Similarly, the impetus for the federal government moving into the arena of medical support for those children eligible for child support was to reduce federal costs in the Medicaid program. This section of the report summarizes major medical child support provisions.

P.L. 95-142, Medicare-Medicaid Anti-fraud and Abuse Amendments (H.R. 3), Enacted October 25, 1977

The first link between child support and medical support came as an attempt to recoup the costs of Medicaid provided to public assistance families under Title XIX of the Social Security Act. Just two years after the creation of the Child Support Enforcement (CSE) (i.e., Title IV-D of the Social Security Act) program, the Medicare/Medicaid Anti-fraud and Abuse Amendments of 1977 established a medical support enforcement program that allowed states to require Medicaid applicants to assign their rights to medical support to the state. Further, in an effort to cover children with private insurance instead of public programs, when available, it permitted CSE and Medicaid agencies to enter into cooperative agreements to pursue medical child support assigned to the state. Activities performed by the CSE agency under a cooperative agreement with the Medicaid agency must be funded by the Medicaid agency. The 1977 law also required state CSE agencies to notify Medicaid agencies when private family health coverage was either obtained or discontinued for a Medicaid-eligible person.

P.L. 98-369, the Deficit Reduction Act of 1984 (H.R. 4170), Enacted July 18, 1984

This law mandated states to require that Medicaid applicants assign their rights to medical support to the state (Section 1912(a) of the Social Security Act).

P.L. 98-378, the Child Support Enforcement Amendments of 1984 (H.R. 4325), Enacted August 16, 1984, and Corresponding Regulations

Section 16 of P.L. 98-378 required the HHS Secretary to issue regulations requiring state CSE agencies to petition for inclusion of medical support as part of any new or modified child support order whenever health care coverage is available at "reasonable cost" to the noncustodial parent of a child receiving AFDC, Medicaid, or foster care benefits or services. Federal regulations further stipulated that any employment-related or other group coverage was considered reasonable, under the assumption that health insurance is inexpensive to the employee/noncustodial parent. A 1993 study by Cooper and Johnson that analyzed 1987 data from the Center for Health Expenditures and Insurance Studies indicated that for workers with income below the poverty line and employer-provided family health insurance, 77% of the premium was paid for by the employer.[147]

Regulations

On October 16, 1985, the Office of Child Support Enforcement (OCSE) published regulations amending previous regulations and implementing section 16 of P.L. 98-378. These regulations required state CSE agencies to obtain basic medical support information and provide this information to the state Medicaid agency. The purpose of medical support enforcement is to expand the number of children for whom private health insurance coverage is obtained and thereby reduce Medicaid costs for both the states and the federal government. If the custodial parent does not have satisfactory health insurance coverage, the child support agency must petition the court or administrative authority to include medical support in new or modified support orders, and to also inform the state Medicaid agency of such support orders that include a medical support obligation. The regulations also require CSE agencies to enforce medical support that has been ordered by a court or administrative process. States receive child support matching funds from the federal government at the 66% rate for required medical support activities.[148]

Before these 1985 regulations were issued, medical support activities were pursued by CSE agencies only under optional cooperative agreements with Medicaid agencies. Some of the functions that the CSE agency performed under these agreements included receiving referrals from the Medicaid agency, locating noncustodial parents, establishing paternity, determining whether the noncustodial parent had a health insurance policy or plan that covered the child, obtaining sufficient information about the health insurance policy or plan to permit the filing of a claim with the insurer, filing a claim with the insurer or transmitting the necessary information to the Medicaid agency, securing health insurance coverage through court or administrative order, and recovering amounts necessary to reimburse Medicaid payments.

On September 16, 1988, OCSE issued additional regulations expanding the medical support enforcement provisions. These regulations required the CSE agency to develop criteria to identify existing child support cases that had a high potential for obtaining medical support, and to petition the court or administrative authority to modify support orders to include medical support for these cases even if no other modification was anticipated. The CSE agency was also required to provide the custodial parent with information regarding the health insurance coverage obtained by the noncustodial parent for the child. Moreover, the regulation deleted the condition that CSE agencies may secure health insurance coverage under a cooperative agreement only when it did not reduce the noncustodial parent's ability to pay child support.[149]

P.L. 101-508, the Omnibus Budget Reconciliation Act of 1990 (H.R. 5835), Enacted November 5, 1990

Section 4606 of P.L. 101-508 amended one provision of section 1912(a)(1) of the Social Security Act to provide an exemption from the requirement of cooperating in establishing paternity and obtaining medical support and payments for poverty-level pregnant women described in section 1902(l)(1)(A) of the act. While poverty level pregnant women are exempt from the cooperation requirements in section 1912(a)(1)(B), these individuals are required to comply with similar provisions in sections 1912(a)(1) (A) and (C). In order to reconcile this apparent inconsistency, the exemption in section 1912(a)(1)(B) has been interpreted by the federal CSE agency (OCSE) as applying only to the father of a child born out of wedlock and entities whose liability derives from the father (e.g., the father's insurer). Therefore, poverty-level pregnant women may not be required as a condition of Medicaid eligibility to cooperate with the state in establishing paternity or in obtaining support and payments for medical care from, or derived from, the father of the child born out of wedlock. The poverty-level pregnant woman is still required to assign her rights, and the rights of any other person eligible for Medicaid for whom she can legally make an assignment, to the state for support and payment of medical care from any third party. She must also cooperate with the state and provide information to be used in pursuing any other third party that may be liable for care and services under the plan.[150]

P.L. 103-66, the Omnibus Budget Reconciliation Act of 1993 (H.R. 2264), Enacted August 10, 1993

Before late 1993, employees covered under their employers' health care plans generally could provide coverage to children only if the children lived with them. However, as a result of divorce proceedings, employees often lost custody of their children but were nonetheless required to provide their health care coverage. While the employee would be obliged to follow the court's directive, the employer that sponsored the employee's health care plan was under no similar obligation. Even if the court ordered the employer to continue health care coverage for the nonresident child of their employee, the employer was under no legal obligation to do so.

Aware of this situation, Congress took the following legislative actions in the Omnibus Budget Reconciliation Act of 1993 (P.L. 103-66):

1. Insurers were prohibited from denying enrollment of a child under the health insurance plan of the child's parent on the grounds that (a) the child was born out of wedlock, (b) is not claimed as a dependent on the parent's federal income tax return, or (c) does not reside with the parent or in the insurer's service area.

2. In any case in which a parent is required by court order to provide health coverage for a child and the child is otherwise eligible for family coverage through the insurer, insurers and employers were required:
    - to permit the parent, without regard to any enrollment season restrictions, to enroll the child under such family coverage,
    - to allow the custodial parent or the Medicaid agency to enroll the child in the noncustodial parent's health plan when the noncustodial parent has family coverage but fails to provide health insurance coverage for a dependent child, and
    - with respect to employers only, not to dis-enroll the child unless there is satisfactory written evidence that the order is no longer in effect or the child is or will be enrolled in comparable health coverage through another insurer that will take effect not later than the effective date of the disenrollment.
3. Employers doing business in the state, if they offer health insurance and if a child support order is in effect, were required to withhold from the employee's compensation the employee's share of premiums for health insurance and to pay that share to the insurer. The HHS Secretary may provide by regulation for such exceptions to this requirement (and other requirements described above that apply to employers) as the Secretary determines necessary to ensure compliance with an order, or with the limits on withholding that are specified in section 303(b) of the Consumer Credit Protection Act.
4. Insurers were prohibited from imposing requirements on a state agency acting as an agent or assignee of an individual eligible for Medicaid that are different from requirements applicable to an agent or assignee of any other individual.
5. Insurers were required to, in the case of a child who has coverage through the insurer of a noncustodial parent: (a) provide the custodial parent with the information necessary for the child to obtain benefits; (b) permit the custodial parent (or provider, with the custodial parent's approval) to submit claims for covered services without the approval of the noncustodial parent; and (c) make payment on claims directly to the custodial parent, the provider, or the state agency.
6. The state Medicaid agency was permitted to garnish the wages, salary, or other employment income of, and to withhold state tax refunds to, any person who (1) is required by court or administrative order to provide health insurance coverage to an individual eligible for

Medicaid; (2) has received payment from a third party for the costs of medical services to that individual; and (2) has not reimbursed either the individual or the provider. The amount subject to garnishment or withholding is the amount required to reimburse the state agency for expenditures for medical services provided under the Medicaid program. Claims for current or past due child support take priority over any claims for the costs of medical services.

P.L. 104-193, the Personal Responsibility and Work Opportunity Reconciliation Act of 1996 (H.R. 3734), Enacted August 22, 1996

Under the 1996 welfare reform legislation, the definition of "medical child support order" in the Employee Retirement Income Security Act (ERISA) was expanded to clarify that any judgment, decree, or order that is issued by a court or by an administrative process has the force and effect of law. In addition, the 1996 welfare reform law stipulated that all orders enforced by the state CSE agency must include a provision for health care coverage. If the noncustodial parent changes jobs and the new employer provides health coverage, the state must send notice of required coverage to the new employer; the notice must serve to enroll the child in a health plan of the new employer. (Before enactment of P.L. 104-193, families who were not receiving public assistance benefits could choose not to seek medical support.)

P.L. 105-200, the Child Support Performance and Incentive Act of 1998 (H.R. 3130), Enacted July 16, 1998

P.L. 105-200 provided a uniform manner for states to inform employers about their obligation to enroll the children of noncustodial parents in employer-sponsored health plans. It required the CSE agency to use a standardized "National Medical Support Notice" (developed by HHS and the Department of Labor) to communicate to employers the issuance of a medical support order. Employers were required to accept the form as a "Qualified Medical Support Order" under ERISA. States were required to begin using the national medical support notice in October 2001, although many states had to delay implementation until enactment of required state enabling legislation. An appropriately completed national medical support notice is considered to be a "Qualified Medical Child Support Order" and as such must be honored by the employer's group health plan.

P.L. 105-200 also called for the joint establishment of a Medical Support Working Group by the Secretaries of HHS and Labor to identify impediments to the effective enforcement of medical support by state CSE agencies and to submit to the Secretaries of HHS and Labor a report containing recommendations addressing the identified impediments.

In consultation with state CSE directors and representatives of children potentially eligible for medical support, the HHS Secretary was directed to develop a performance measure based on the effectiveness of states in establishing and enforcing medical support obligations, and to make recommendations for the incorporation of the measure in a revenue neutral manner into the Child Support Incentive Payment System. These recommendations were due no later than October 1, 1999.

P.L. 106-394, the Federal Employees Health Benefits Children's Equity Act of 2000 (H.R. 2842), Enacted October 30, 2000

P.L. 106-394 provides federal agencies authority under the Federal Employees Health Benefits Children's Equity Act of 2000 to enroll an employee and his or her family in the Federal Employee Health Benefits Program (FEHBP) when a state court or administrative authority orders the employee to provide health insurance coverage for a child of the employee but the employee fails or refuses to provide the coverage. Federal agencies may also enforce a child support order providing for direct income assignment (i.e., an amount of money for medical purposes as specified in the order).[151]

If the employee is not enrolled for any FEHBP coverage, the agency employing office must enroll the dependents and/or the employee in the standard option of the Blue Cross/Blue Shield Service Benefit Plan. If the employee has a self-only enrollment in a fee-for-service plan, the agency must change the enrollment to self-and-family in the same option of the same plan. Authorized enrollment changes may be processed retroactively, if necessary, to comply with the effective date of the court or administrative order. The Federal agency employer will receive a National Medical Support Notice from the state child support enforcement agency and will be required to notify the plan administrator to enroll the children in an insurance plan. Upon enrollment, the Federal agency employer will withhold premiums from the employee's income. This order may be subsequent to, or in conjunction with, an order to withhold a monetary child support obligation.[152]

P.L. 109-171, the Deficit Reduction Act of 2005 (S. 1932), Enacted February 8, 2006, and Final Regulations

P.L. 109-171 required child support orders enforced by the CSE program to include a provision for medical child support. It required states to consider either or both parents' access to health insurance and permits enforcement of medical child support against both parents. P.L. 109-171 defines "medical support" to include both health insurance (coverage under a health insurance plan, including payment of premiums, co-payments, and deductibles) and payment for children's medical expenses. If health insurance is not available, states may require both parents to share the cost of their children's medical expenses.

Regulations

On July 21, 2008, the Administration for Children and Families at HHS issued final regulations related to medical child support. The regulations include both the Deficit Reduction Act changes and recommendations by the Medical Child Support Working Group (MCSWG). Among other actions, the final regulations stipulate that cash medical support or private health insurance is considered reasonable in amount if the cost to the obligated parent does not exceed 5% of his or her gross income or, at state option, a reasonable alternative income-based numeric standard defined in state child support guidelines. The final regulations also require the state CSE agency to inform the Medicaid agency when there is a new or modified court or administrative order for child support that includes health insurance and/or cash medical support in the case of a child who is a Medicaid applicant or recipient. Also, the state CSE agency is required to communicate periodically with the Medicaid agency to determine if there have been lapses in Medicaid coverage for Medicaid applicants or recipients. To the extent that medical support has been assigned to the state, medical support collections are forwarded to the Medicaid agency for distribution in accordance with federal regulations. Otherwise, the amount is forwarded to the family.[153]

APPENDIX B. MEDICAL SUPPORT COVERAGE OF CHILDREN

The following medical support data are drawn from the CSE program's annual data reports to Congress.[154] It is the only available state data on medical child support. States submit medical support data to the federal Office of Child Support Enforcement (OCSE), but the data are not subject to an audit to determine if they are complete and reliable. Also, because medical support establishment allows states to initiate legal medical support orders before determining whether the health insurance is affordable, state CSE agencies are severely hampered in successfully enforcing medical child support orders in cases in which a medical support order is established but the health insurance is not considered affordable by federal/state standards. Thus, one reason why coverage may not be provided as ordered (i.e., why enforcement rates of medical support are low) may be because it is not available to the obligated parent at a reasonable rate. There is little that the CSE agency can do to enforce the existing medical support order in these circumstances. Thus, the medical support data in the following two tables should be used with caution.

With regard to **Table B-1,** information from the state CSE programs indicates the following for FY2011:

- There were 15.8 million CSE cases.[155] As mentioned earlier the services provided by the CSE program include among other things, locating noncustodial parents, establishing paternity, establishing child support orders, and collecting child support payments.
- There were 12.8 million child support orders established. Some of the reasons why child support orders are not established for all cases are the following: the noncustodial parent's whereabouts is unknown, paternity has not been established, and/or income and resource information concerning the noncustodial parent has not yet been determined.
- There were 2.8 million arrearages-only cases in which child support orders were established. Arrearages-only cases are cases in which the noncustodial parent does not owe any current child support but still owes past-due child support (i.e., the noncustodial parent did not pay the entire amount of child support owed in a prior given month). In accordance with CSE accounting procedures, cases with arrearages

only are subtracted from the number of cases with an order established in determining medical support statistics.

- There were 10.0 million cases with child support orders established if the arrearages-only cases are excluded.
- Medical child support was ordered in 8.1 million of the 10.0 million cases in which child support was established (81% of the cases).
- The medical support order was complied with in 3.3 million of those 10.0 million cases (33% of the cases).

As indicated in the body of this report, the existence of medical support (whether or not it is complied with) is not directly related to whether a child has health care coverage. In many cases in which the custodial parent has private health insurance or has enrolled her or his children in a publicly-funded health care program (such as Medicaid or CHIP), there might not be a medical support order.

Table B-1. Percent of Child Support Cases with Orders in Which Medical Support is Ordered,Versus Ordered and Provided: FY2009, FY2010, and FY2011

	FY2009		FY2010		FY2011	
	Percent of Child Support Cases with Orders in Which Medical Support Is ...					
	Ordered	Provided	Ordered	Provided	Ordered	Provided
Alabama	74.6%	22.7%	79.1%	34.7%	82.1%	41.5%
Alaska	94.6%	39.5%	94.3%	38.0%	94.5%	41.1%
Arizona	85.5%	26.7%	85.9%	29.9%	86.7%	28.0%
Arkansas	75.2%	26.0%	76.7%	26.3%	77.9%	27.2%
California	90.5%	48.3%	93.0%	52.0%	93.1%	53.8%
Colorado	85.3%	40.1%	86.4%	42.1%	86.8%	42.5%
Connecticut	89.9%	23.1%	90.2%	21.8%	90.9%	21.2%
Delaware	137.3%	35.3%	143.1%	37.1%	149.2%	40.5%
District of Columbia	62.4%	27.3%	62.4%	27.4%	63.6%	28.6%
Florida	64.7%	6.4%	67.7%	7.2%	68.6%	8.5%
Georgia	77.6%	21.1%	76.9%	21.3%	75.3%	21.5%
Guam	38.0%	15.1%	40.6%	16.8%	41.9%	17.3%
Hawaii	79.7%	30.7%	80.0%	31.4%	80.2%	31.6%
Idaho	87.4%	20.2%	89.9%	34.9%	89.8%	33.8%
Illinois	51.2%	9.8%	50.9%	11.9%	51.6%	12.3%
Indiana	73.4%	11.1%	74.2%	10.4%	74.2%	5.0%
Iowa	87.5%	38.4%	88.9%	38.9%	89.2%	40.5%
Kansas	85.5%	20.8%	87.4%	20.9%	88.8%	21.4%

Table B-1. (Continued)

	FY2009		FY2010		FY2011	
	Percent of Child Support Cases with Orders in Which Medical Support Is ...					
	Ordered	**Provided**	**Ordered**	**Provided**	**Ordered**	**Provided**
Kentucky	75.4%	18.5%	77.8%	20.7%	79.5%	21.9%
Louisiana	94.9%	25.5%	94.7%	27.1%	94.5%	28.8%
Maine	91.7%	12.9%	92.9%	14.2%	93.7%	14.0%
Maryland	68.9%	NA	70.3%	28.3%	73.1%	27.7%
Massachusetts	58.3%	30.8%	71.3%	33.2%	67.3%	33.3%
Michigan	91.3%	44.4%	88.4%	46.7%	87.0%	47.7%
Minnesota	80.7%	43.0%	74.1%	38.7%	75.1%	38.4%
Mississippi	45.1%	11.5%	41.8%	10.0%	43.3%	9.8%
Missouri	86.3%	25.6%	87.4%	25.0%	88.1%	25.4%
Montana	90.7%	46.8%	91.6%	45.7%	92.1%	46.6%
Nebraska	88.2%	39.4%	87.6%	40.2%	86.2%	40.9%
Nevada	69.2%	24.3%	69.2%	24.7%	90.0%	24.6%
New Hampshire	91.2%	8.1%	92.5%	12.2%	93.6%	13.3%
New Jersey	65.3%	14.3%	62.0%	13.4%	63.8%	13.9%
New Mexico	82.9%	27.4%	83.7%	27.8%	84.9%	29.4%
New York	68.0%	22.2%	70.9%	23.3%	72.7%	23.7%
North Carolina	80.8%	20.5%	81.8%	19.8%	82.1%	19.3%
North Dakota	98.5%	53.7%	98.0%	53.8%	98.1%	52.8%
Ohio	73.1%	36.3%	75.7%	35.0%	77.8%	34.0%
Oklahoma	88.3%	23.1%	89.3%	22.2%	89.9%	25.1%
Oregon	86.1%	38.2%	87.1%	37.8%	87.2%	37.0%
Pennsylvania	86.6%	73.7%	88.6%	77.5%	90.4%	79.8%
Puerto Rico	9.9%	0.4%	12.5%	0.5%	15.0%	0.6%
Rhode Island	78.8%	54.1%	78.4%	56.8%	80.8%	59.4%
South Carolina	55.4%	4.4%	60.6%	3.6%	64.2%	2.9%
South Dakota	88.8%	37.0%	90.8%	40.0%	91.3%	41.0%
Tennessee	74.9%	15.5%	77.4%	14.8%	80.1%	15.6%
Texas	91.6%	60.7%	92.2%	61.5%	93.6%	63.7%
Utah	95.4%	54.0%	95.6%	50.0%	95.4%	48.9%
Vermont	95.0%	20.1%	95.2%	19.4%	95.5%	18.6%
Virgin Islands	66.6%	10.2%	68.1%	13.0%	68.9%	14.5%
Virginia	80.4%	17.6%	84.2%	23.5%	85.9%	23.7%
Washington	91.3%	23.7%	91.2%	21.2%	91.1%	19.3%
West Virginia	81.0%	14.3%	83.8%	16.3%	83.3%	16.2%
Wisconsin	96.2%	35.6%	97.0%	34.8%	97.0%	34.2%
Wyoming	75.7%	35.3%	80.9%	35.2%	80.9%	31.5%
Total	**78.7%**	**31.6%**	**79.7%**	**32.5%**	**80.7%**	**32.9%**

Source: Table prepared by the Congressional Research Service, based on data from the Department of Health and Human Services, Office of Child Support Enforcement (see Table 41 in FY2009 Annual Child Support Report to Congress, Table P-33 in the FY2010 Preliminary Child Support Report, and Table P-33 in FY2011 Preliminary Child Support Report).

Notes: In FY2011, there were 15,831,904 CSE cases. In 81% of those cases, a child support order was established. The primary reason why there is no child support order is that paternity had not been established. Another reason might be that the whereabouts of the noncustodial parent was unknown. As seen in the table above, in FY2011, the nationwide total shows that 81% of child support cases with a child support order included medical child support. The table also shows that the medical support order was complied with in 33% of those cases.

N.A. = Not Available.

Health insurance coverage is the primary form of medical support. In FY2001, 93% of medical support orders stipulated health insurance coverage. In FY2011, the percentage was 88%. The information in **Table B-2** is a subset of the information in **Table B-1**. The compliance rates for medical support in the form of health insurance are similar to medical support compliance in general. In FY2011, medical support orders that stipulated the provision of health insurance coverage applied to 55% of all CSE cases that had a child support order, and as mentioned 88% of cases with a medical support order. Health insurance coverage was provided as ordered in 31% of those cases.[156] (See **Table B-2**.)

Table B-2. Percent of Child Support Cases with a Health Insurance Order Where Health Insurance Was Provided as Ordered: FY2001 and FY2011

	Percent of Child Support Cases with a Health Insurance Order Where Health Insurance was Provided as Ordered	
State	FY2001	FY2011
Alabama	0.7%	13.1%
Alaska	31.7%	41.5%
Arizona	1.6%	78.0%
Arkansas	16.9%	26.5%
California	22.6%	23.7%
Colorado	8.3%	39.0%
Connecticut	16.7%	20.3%
Delaware	2.6%	27.2%
District of Columbia	0.0%	34.4%

Table B-2. (Continued)

	Percent of Child Support Cases with a Health Insurance Order Where Health Insurance was Provided as Ordered	
State	FY2001	FY2011
Florida	3.6%	9.9%
Georgia	18.7%	26.3%
Guam	11.2%	40.6%
Hawaii	13.4%	35.5%
Idaho	11.0%	18.6%
Illinois	27.1%	22.1%
Indiana	1.1%	6.2%
Iowa	22.9%	36.3%
Kansas	9.2%	24.9%
Kentucky	5.0%	27.7%
Louisiana	0.6%	30.4%
Maine	4.5%	13.7%
Maryland	39.2%	33.7%
Massachusetts	2.3%	48.2%
Michigan	15.9%	39.2%
Minnesota	35.8%	56.6%
Mississippi	18.2%	69.2%
Missouri	12.0%	22.6%
Montana	27.0%	51.8%
Nebraska	0.0%	47.3%
Nevada	5.3%	24.5%
New Hampshire	9.3%	16.7%
New Jersey	28.0%	21.8%
New Mexico	12.7%	30.8%
New York	0.0%	N.A.
North Carolina	31.5%	23.7%
North Dakota	40.8%	39.4%
Ohio	85.6%	65.3%
Oklahoma	0.0%	26.2%
Oregon	22.2%	36.9%
Pennsylvania	30.9%	84.2%
Puerto Rico	37.2%	30.8%
Rhode Island	19.5%	50.2%
South Carolina	8.4%	12.1%
South Dakota	21.7%	32.3%
Tennessee	14.1%	17.0%

	Percent of Child Support Cases with a Health Insurance Order Where Health Insurance was Provided as Ordered	
State	FY2001	FY2011
Texas	6.8%	48.6%
Utah	48.0%	46.5%
Vermont	76.1%	85.6%
Virgin Islands	NA	18.5%
Virginia	8.7%	27.2%
Washington	25.7%	32.7%
West Virginia	7.2%	16.5%
Wisconsin	21.4%	N.A.
Wyoming	13.8%	22.9%
Total	**17.9%**	**30.5%**

Source: Table prepared by the Congressional Research Service, based on data from the Department of Health and Human Services, Office of Child Support Enforcement (see Table 21 in the Annual Statistical Report for FY2001 and Table P-34 in the FY2011 Preliminary Child Support Report).

Notes: This table examines a subset of medical support (i.e., health insurance coverage). Health insurance coverage is the primary form of medical support. The nationwide total shows that in FY2011, child support orders that specifically required that health insurance be provided for the child(ren) in question were complied with 30.5% of the time.

N.A. = Not Available.

End Notes

[1] See http://www.rasmussenreports.com/public_content/archive/ mood_of_america_archive/ importance_of_issues/ economy_health_care_still_top_voters_list_of_important_issues.

[2] For general information on the CSE program, see CRS Report RS22380, *Child Support Enforcement: Program Basics*, by Carmen Solomon-Fears. The CSE program was established as Title IV-D of the Social Security Act in 1975 pursuant to P.L. 93-647.

[3] P.L. 109-171 amended Section 452(f) of the Social Security Act to include a definition of medical support.

[4] For state-specific information regarding state statutes on medical support and contact information, see the following webpage: http://www.acf.hhs.gov/programs/css/resource/ state-medical-support-contacts-and-information.

[5] CSE agency staff carry out this duty by determining the employment status of the noncustodial parent and whether health insurance coverage is available for his or her children. If such coverage is available, the CSE agency notifies the employer of the employee's medical child support obligation and the employer's responsibility to enroll the children of the employee in its health care plan. In practice, however, some CSE agencies do not verify availability of affordable employer-sponsored coverage before establishing a medical support order. They sometimes use the National Medical Support Notice as a discovery tool, and request that the employer enroll the child if affordable coverage is available.

[6] Department of Health and Human Services, Administration for Children and Families, Office of Child Support Enforcement, *21 Million Children's Health: Our Shared Responsibility*, The Medical Child Support Working Group, June 2000.

[7] Although it is a separate expense, many states include medical child support costs in the calculation of the regular child support order.

[8] This report uses the terms "affordable" and "reasonable" interchangeable. However, "reasonable" is the legal term that is defined in CSE regulations.

[9] In FY2011, there were 15,831,904 CSE cases. In 81% of those cases, a child support order was established. The primary reason why there is no child support order is that paternity had not been established. Another reason might be that the whereabouts of the noncustodial parent was unknown. (**Note:** OCSE defines a CSE "case" as a noncustodial parent (mother, father, or putative/alleged father) who is now or eventually may be obligated under law for the support of a child or children receiving services under the CSE program. If the noncustodial parent owes support for two children by different women, that would be considered two cases; if both children have the same mother that would be considered one case.)

[10] Department of Health and Human Services, Administration for Children and Families, Office of Child Support Enforcement, *FY2011 Annual Report to Congress*, October 1, 2012, Table 33.

[11] According to some CSE experts, the Department of Agriculture report entitled, *Expenditures on Children by Families* is one of the reports most widely used by states in developing their child support guidelines. The report can be found at http://www.cnpp.usda.gov/Publications/CRC/crc2011.pdf).

[12] Department of Health and Human Services, Administration for Children and Families, Office of Child Support Enforcement, 2007 Best Practices, *Medicaid Cost Savings-Massachusetts*, January 1, 2007.

[13] The Congressional Budget Office (CBO) cost estimates of the ACA coverage provisions indicate that many more people will be insured given the ACA as opposed to without the ACA. Even though it is projected that there will be more coverage, CBO expects that there will be 44 million uninsured non-elderly individuals in 2014 and 29 million such persons in 2017 (includes unauthorized immigrants and individuals who are eligible but not enrolled in Medicaid). See Congressional Budget Office, *CBO's February 2013 Estimate of the Effects of the Affordable Care Act on Health Insurance Coverage*, February 5, 2013.

[14] CRS Report R41664, *ACA: A Brief Overview of the Law, Implementation, and Legal Challenges*, coordinated by C. Stephen Redhead, July 3, 2012, p. 1.

[15] The regulations implementing this provision recognize that state CSE agencies generally do not establish child support orders. Rather many orders are established under a judicial, quasi-judicial, or administrative process outside of the CSE agency. When orders are established through the courts, state CSE agencies can petition but cannot require inclusion of medical support provisions. State child support guidelines are also required to provide for the inclusion of medical support, but judges and administrative officials can deviate from those guidelines if appropriate. (For a discussion of establishment provisions, see *Administrative and Judicial Processes for Establishing Child Support Orders*, the Lewin Group for the Office of Child Support Enforcement, Administration for Children and Families, Department of Health and Human Services, June 20002, accessed at http://www.lewin.com/~/media/Lewin/Site_Sections/Publications/2609.pdf. For information on the requirements to petition for inclusion of medical support, see 45 C.F.R. Part 303.31(b)).

[16] The CSE program is not required to pursue medical support coverage through the custodial parent's employer. Federal regulations at 45 C.F.R. 303.32 stipulate: "*States must have laws, in accordance with section 466(a)(19) of the Act, requiring procedures specified under paragraph (c) of this section for the use, where appropriate, of the National Medical Support Notice (NMSN), to enforce the provision of health care coverage for children of noncustodial parents and, at State option, custodial parents who are required to provide*

health care coverage through an employment- related group health plan pursuant to a child support order and for whom the employer is known to the State agency."

[17] 45 C.F.R. §303.31(a)(3).

[18] Note that in most employment-based health insurance coverage, the employee must enroll in order to cover his or her dependents. Thus, if an employee has not enrolled, he or she will have to do so (if so order by the CSE agency or a court) to obtain ordered coverage for his or her children. (Source: *Federal Register*, vol. 73, no. 140, July 21, 2008, p. 42426.)

[19] 42 U.S.C §666(a)(19). Note that the NMSN is a vehicle for providing health insurance coverage. It has no applicability to any other medical support provisions.

[20] The term "cost-sharing" has different meanings in the programs discussed in this report. In the CSE program cost- sharing refers to the joint responsibility of both parents to pay for their children's health-related expenses. In the Medicaid and CHIP programs, beneficiaries may encounter two types of out-of-pocket expenditures (1) participant- related cost-sharing, usually in the form of monthly premiums, whether or not services are utilized, and (2) service- related cost-sharing, which consist of payments made directly to providers at the time of service delivery. For more information, see CRS Report RS22578, *Medicaid Cost-Sharing Under the Deficit Reduction Act of 2005 (DRA)*, by Elicia J. Herz.

[21] CRS Report R42663, *Health Insurance Exchanges Under the Patient Protection and Affordable Care Act (ACA)*, by Bernadette Fernandez and Annie L. Mach, October 10, 2012.

[22] National Council of State Legislatures, *Child Support Administration*, updated September 2012.

[23] As noted throughout this report, states have the authority to send the NMSN to an employer before it is determined that the health insurance provided by the employer is affordable to the employee based on federal/state standards.

[24] 45 C.F.R. §303.32(c).

[25] *Federal Register*, vol. 73, no. 140, Department of Health and Human Services, Office of Child Support Enforcement, "Child Support Enforcement Program: Medical Support," final regulation, July 21, 2008, pp. 42416-42442.

[26] Federal law (42 U.S.C §667) requires that all states have child support guidelines (a calculation of how much a parent should contribute to the child's financial support). Those guidelines must be used to establish child support orders unless it is shown, in writing, that doing so is not in the best interest of the child. Most state guidelines consider the needs of the child, other dependents, and the ability of the parents to pay. In addition, federal law (42 U.S.C.§666(a)(19)) requires that every child support order handled by the CSE program include a provision for medical support of children.

[27] 45 C.F.R. 302.56(c)(3).

[28] 45 C.F.R. §303.31.

[29] For state-specific information regarding medical support on the following topics: (1) contact information, (2) priority for withholding, (3) state statute on medical support, and (4) reasonable cost definition, see http://www.acf.hhs.gov/ programs/css/resource/state-medical-support-contacts-and-information.

[30] Department of Health and Human Services, Office of Child Support Enforcement, *Handbook on Child Support Enforcement*, 2008, p. 23.

[31] P.L. 109-171 (the Deficit Reduction Act of 2005) acknowledged that medical coverage had value regardless of its source. The emphasis on obtaining private health care coverage exclusively from noncustodial parents was dismissed in favor of examining the range of health care options and choosing the one that would serve each child best. Many advocates maintain that a child may be better off getting health care coverage under a custodial parent's health insurance because access to services and consistency of coverage are less problematic.

[32] In response to the requirement to include medical support, many state child support guidelines indicate that medical support must be a part of the order. However, often this is done by

adding the following type of phrase, especially when health insurance is not currently available, "the noncustodial parent (name) shall provide health insurance for (name) when available through his/her employer at a reasonable cost." This type of general requirement can result in many exceptions and/or contingencies. For example, assume health insurance is ordered. If notification of employment is found through the New Hire reporting system or other information sources, the Medical Support Notice goes out. If the employer responds that the parent has or is eligible for family coverage and the cost is reasonable, the child can be enrolled. Moreover, sometimes an order may say that either or both parents shall provide medical support which adds another layer of complexity to the enforcement of medical support.

[33] By requiring the states to establish child support guidelines, the federal government expected to accomplish four main goals, each goal corresponding to the perceived problems of the common law method of determining child support: (1) increase the adequacy of child support awards; (2) increase the consistency and predictability of child support awards; (3) increase compliance through perceived fairness of child support awards; and (4) increase the ease of administration of child support cases. States generally use one of three basic types of guidelines to determine award amounts: "Income shares" which is based on the combined income of both parents; "percentage of income" in which the number of eligible children is used to determine a percentage of the noncustodial parents' income to be paid in child support; and "Melson-Delaware" which provides a minimum self-support reserve for parents before the cost of rearing the children is prorated between the parents to determine the child support award amount.

[34] *Federal Register*, vol. 73, no. 140; Department of Health and Human Services, Administration for Children and Families, Office of Child Support Enforcement, "Child Support Enforcement: Medical Support" (Final Regulation), July 21, 2008, p. 42419.

[35] Ibid.

[36] In contrast, during FY2001, health insurance coverage was ordered in 49% of all CSE cases that had a child support order, but the health insurance order was complied with in only 18% of those cases.

[37] Department of Health and Human Services, Administration for Children and Families , Office of Child Support Enforcement, *Notice of Changes to the OCSE-157 Form regarding Medical Support*, AT-11-10, October 17, 2011.

[38] For more information, see CRS Report RS22889, *The National Directory of New Hires*, by Carmen Solomon-Fears, *The National Directory of New Hires*, by Carmen Solomon-Fears.

[39] Contrary to its name, the National Directory of New Hires includes more than just information on new employees. It is a database that includes information on (1) all newly hired employees, compiled from state reports (and reports from federal employers), (2) the quarterly wage reports of existing employees (in Unemployment Compensation (UC)-covered employment), and (3) unemployment compensation claims. This Directory was originally established in 1996 (P.L. 104-193) to help states locate noncustodial parents living in a different state so that child support payments could be withheld from that parent's paycheck.

[40] The 1996 welfare reform law (P.L. 104-193) also required states to have automated registries of child support orders containing records of each case in which CSE services are being provided, and each support order established or modified on or after October 1, 1998. Local registries may be linked to form the state registry. The state child support case registry includes a record of the child support owed under the order, child support arrearages, interest or late penalty charges, amounts of child support collected, amounts distributed, child's date of birth, and any liens imposed. The state child support case registry also includes standardized information on both parents, such as name, SSN, date of birth, and case identification number. P.L. 104-193 also required the establishment of a federal child support case registry. Both federal directories (i.e., the federal child support case registry

and the NDNH) consist of abstracts of information from the state directories and are located in the Federal Parent Locator Service (FPLS) in HHS.

[41] Performance, Service, Integrity (PSI), *21st Century Prototype: Optimizing Collaboration Between Child Support and Medicaid/CHIP Programs to Offset State Expenditures, and Achieve a Continuum of Health Care Coverage for Children*, January 4, 2005.

[42] A comprehensive list of all federal agencies including the agency name, medical support notice address, and contact information can be found at http://www.acf.hhs.gov/ sites/default/files/ programs/css/fa_addresses_for_medical_support_notices.pdf. The current list, posted October 1, 2012, can be used by child support agencies to ensure medical support notices are sent to the appropriate address.

[43] A 1993 amendment (P.L. 103-66) to the Employee Retirement Income Security Act (ERISA) requires employment- based group health plans to extend health care coverage to the children of a parent-employee who is divorced, separated, or never married when ordered to do so by state authorities. Generally, a state court or agency may require an ERISA-covered health plan to provide health benefits coverage to children by issuing a medical child support order. The group health plan must determine whether the medical child support order is "qualified." Such an order is referred to as a Qualified Medical Child Support Order (QMCSO). (Source: http://www.dol.gov/ebsa/publications/qmcso.html.)

[44] ERISA §§3(7), 609(a)(1). See also Department of Labor, Qualified Medical Child Support Orders— http://www.dol.gov/ebsa/publications/qmcso.html.

[45] Performance, Service, Integrity (PSI), *21st Century Prototype: Optimizing Collaboration Between Child Support and Medicaid/SCHIP Programs to Offset State Expenditures, and Achieve a Continuum of Health Care Coverage for Children*, January 4, 2005, p. 5.

[46] Department of Health and Human Services, Administration for Children and Families, Office of Child Support Enforcement, *FY2011 Preliminary Report*, October 1, 2012, p. 4.

[47] Department of Health and Human Services, Administration for Children and Families, Office of Child Support Enforcement, *Child Support Fact Sheet Series*, no. 6, "Health Care Coverage," 2012, p. 2.

[48] CRS Report RL33202, *Medicaid: A Primer*, by Elicia J. Herz, p. 1.

[49] For more information on third party liability (TPL) see http://www.medicaid.gov/Medicaid-CHIP-Program-Information/By-Topics/Eligibility/Downloads/SummaryofFederal RegulatoryRequirements.pdf.

[50] In some circumstances, a child may be enrolled in both a private health insurance plan and also receive Medicaid "wrap-around" benefits if the employer sponsored insurance does not cover some benefit and/or benefit caps are reached. The Medicaid program is generally the payor of last resort. Federal regulation at 42 C.F.R. §433.139(b)(3) indicate that the Medicaid agency must pay the full amount allowed under the agency's payment schedule for the claim and seek reimbursement from any liable third party in the case of prenatal care services, preventive pediatric services, and services provided to a minor for whom the state is enforcing a child support order against a noncustodial parent. Thus, some children are dually enrolled regardless of which parent holds the private coverage for the child.

[51] Section 1931 of the Social Security Act allows adjustment of income and resource standards for inflation and allows states to use less restrictive rules for counting income and resources.

[52] For more information, see CRS Report RL33202, *Medicaid: A Primer*, by Elicia J. Herz, p. 2.

[53] To the extent that medical support has been assigned to the state, medical support collections are forwarded to the Medicaid agency for distribution in accordance with federal regulations. Otherwise, the amount is forwarded to the family.

[54] Section 1912 of the Social Security Act [42 U.S.C. §1396k].

[55] 42 CFR §433.148(b).

[56] Paula Roberts, *Rethinking the Medicaid Child Support Cooperation Requirem*ent, Center for Law and Social Policy, May 2003, pp. 4-7.

[57] Many states prohibit recovery of Medicaid birthing costs based on older studies that indicated that some women who were eligible for Medicaid did not apply because they did not want

to establish paternity or seek child support. In fact, in 1990, Congress eliminated the child support cooperation requirement for certain pregnant women because the requirements were considered a potential barrier to prenatal care for high-risk low-income women who were likely to benefit most from the Medicaid program. It was argued that some low-income pregnant women would not apply for Medicaid out of concern that, if they sought prenatal care, the fathers of their children would be required to pay some or all of a medical bill that the fathers could not afford.

[58] Marguerite Roulet and Michael Rust, *Report on Wisconsin's Medicaid-Supported Birth Cost Recovery Policy*, Center on Fathers, Families, and Public Policy, 2004, p. 6; Department of Health and Human Services, Administration for Children and Families, Office of Child Support Enforcement, *21 Million Children's Health: Our Shared Responsibility*, The Medical Child Support Working Group, June 2000, pp. 3-29 through 3-30.

[59] Department of Health and Human Services, Administration for Children and Families, Office of Child Support Enforcement, Handbook on Child Support Enforcement, Chapter X ("Lessons Learned"), 2005.

[60] 45 C.F.R. §433.147.

[61] 42 U.S.C. §1396k(a)(1)(B) or Section 1902(l)(1)(A) of the Social Security Act.

[62] Paula Roberts, *Rethinking the Medicaid Child Support Cooperation Requirem*ent, Center for Law and Social Policy, May 2003, pp. 6-7.

[63] CRS Report R40226, *P.L. 111-3: The Children's Health Insurance Program Reauthorization Act of 2009*, by Evelyne P. Baumrucker, Elicia J. Herz, and Jane G. Gravelle, January 11, 2012. See also CRS Report R41210, *Medicaid and the State Children's Health Insurance Program (CHIP) Provisions in ACA: Summary and Timeline*, by Evelyne P. Baumrucker et al., January 18, 2012.

[64] Paula Roberts, *Rethinking the Medicaid Child Support Cooperation Requirem*ent, Center for Law and Social Policy, May 2003.

[65] Ibid.

[66] Ibid.

[67] CRS Report R42663, *Health Insurance Exchanges Under the Patient Protection and Affordable Care Act (ACA)*, by Bernadette Fernandez and Annie L. Mach.

[68] See http://healthreform.kff.org/Faq/What-is-a-health-insurance-exchange.aspx.

[69] The ACA provides assistance, for the purchase of exchange coverage, in the form of premium tax credits. (A tax credit is a reduction that is applied to the amount an individual (or family) owes, if any, when filing income taxes.) Premium tax credits are advanceable, meaning instead of having to wait until after the end of the tax year to receive the credit, the individual may receive the payments in advance to coincide with when insurance premiums are due (usually on a monthly basis). In addition, the ACA provides cost-sharing subsidies to certain individuals to help them pay costs related to the use of health services. (Cost-sharing generally refers to costs that an individual must pay when using services that are covered under the health plan that the person is enrolled in; common forms of cost-sharing include copayments and deductibles.) For additional information, see CRS Report R42663, *Health Insurance Exchanges Under the Patient Protection and Affordable Care Act (ACA)*, by Bernadette Fernandez and Annie L. Mach.

[70] Pursuant to section 1401 of P.L. 111-148 (ACA), the health insurance exchange premium credit can only apply to a dependent child if that child is claimed as a dependent for federal income tax purposes by the parent filing for the premium credit.

[71] Kaiser Commission on Medicaid and the Uninsured, *Explaining Health Reform: The New Rules for Determining Income Under Medicaid in 2014*, June 2011, p. 4.

[72] Pursuant to the P.L. 98-369 (the Deficit Reduction Act of 1984), the personal tax exemption for a dependent child generally belongs to the custodial parent. In order for the noncustodial parent to receive the exemption, the custodial parent must sign a written declaration that he or she will not claim the child as a dependent. Moreover, the written declaration must be attached to the income tax return of the noncustodial parent claiming the tax exemption.

[73] National Conference of State Legislatures, *Child Support Administration*, updated September 2012. See also Center for Policy Research, *Medical Child Support: Strategies Implemented by States*, Submitted to Texas Office of the Attorney General Division of Child Support, June 16, 2009.

[74] For additional information on coordination between the CSE and Medicaid Programs, see Department of Health and Human Services, Administration for Children and Families, Office of Child Support Enforcement, *Guidance on Referral of Medicaid Cases to Title IV-D Child Support Enforcement Agencies*, Information Memorandum, IM-2008- 03, April 22, 2008.

[75] Paula Roberts, *Rethinking the Medicaid Child Support Cooperation Requirem*ent, Center for Law and Social Policy, May 2003, p. 1.

[76] It is important to note that Medicaid is often the program of last resort, so if a custodial parent is barred from Medicaid because of noncooperation, she or he may not have any other health care coverage options. Beginning in January 2014, such parents may have the option of the health insurance exchanges.

[77] Pat Redmond (The Center on Budget and Policy Priorities), *A Medicaid Perspective on Medical Support Cooperation: A Study of Procedures in Five States*, The Kaiser Commission on Medicaid and the Uninsured, April 2005, p. 1.

[78] Paula Roberts, *Rethinking the Medicaid Child Support Cooperation Requirement*, Center for Law and Social Policy, May 2003, p. 10.

[79] Rules for counting income for Medicaid vary from state to state, with some states allowing disregards and deductions that are not allowed in others. The adoption of MAGI, which is based on adjusted gross income as defined in the Internal Revenue Code §36B(d)(2), will standardize the calculation of income across the nation.

[80] Kaiser Commission on Medicaid and the Uninsured, *Explaining Health Reform: The New Rules for Determining Income Under Medicaid in 2014*, June 2011, p. 2.

[81] CRS Report R41210, *Medicaid and the State Children's Health Insurance Program (CHIP) Provisions in ACA: Summary and Timeline*, by Evelyne P. Baumrucker et al., p. 13-14.

[82] Department of Health and Human Services, Centers for Medicare & Medicaid Services, 77 *Federal Register*, final rule, interim final rule, March 23, 2012, pages 17143 -17217. Available at https://federalregister.gov/a/2012-6560. The Medicaid eligibility final rule is effective January 1, 2014.

[83] Department of Health and Human Services, Centers for Medicare & Medicaid Services, *Verification of Access to Employer-Sponsored Coverage Bulletin*, Center for Consumer Information and Insurance Oversight, April 26, 2012.

[84] Pat Redmond (The Center on Budget and Policy Priorities), *A Medicaid Perspective on Medical Support Cooperation: A Study of Procedures in Five States*, The Kaiser Commission on Medicaid and the Uninsured, April 2005, p. 5.

[85] CRS Report R41159, *Summary of Potential Employer Penalties Under the Patient Protection and Affordable Care Act (PPACA)*, by Janemarie Mulvey.

[86] CRS Report R42378, *Child Welfare: Health Care Needs of Children in Foster Care and Related Federal Issues*, by Evelyne P. Baumrucker et al., p. 37.

[87] CRS Report R42663, *Health Insurance Exchanges Under the Patient Protection and Affordable Care Act (ACA)*, by Bernadette Fernandez and Annie L. Mach, p. 26.

[88] CRS Report R42378, *Child Welfare: Health Care Needs of Children in Foster Care and Related Federal Issues*, by Evelyne P. Baumrucker et al., July 24, 2012, p. 29.

[89] Note that undocumented immigrants are excluded from ACA requirements. In addition, individuals eligible but not enrolled in Medicaid are not subject to the individual health coverage mandate because of low income.

[90] U.S. Census Bureau, *Current Population Reports* P60-243, "Income, Poverty, and Health Insurance Coverage in the United States: 2011," by Carmen DeNavas-Walt, Bernadette D. Proctor, and Jessica C. Smith, September 2012, p. 22. [91] Ibid., p. 27.

[92] Stacey McMorrow, Genevieve Kenney, Allison Cook, and Christine Coyer (of the Urban Institute), *Health Care Coverage and Medicaid/Chip Eligibility for Child Support Eligible Children*, Department of Health and Human Services, Office of the Assistant Secretary for Planning and Evaluation, ASPE Research Brief, July 2011, p. 3.

[93] These were U.S. children age 18 and under who had at least one parent living outside the household (2008 data). According to OCSE data, in FY2011, there were 17.3 million children in the CSE program. The CSE program handles about 60% of all child support cases; the remaining cases are handled by private attorneys, collection agencies, or through mutual agreements between the parents. Also, CSE children can be older than age 18.

[94] Stacey McMorrow, Genevieve Kenney, Allison Cook, and Christine Coyer (of the Urban Institute), *Health Care Coverage and Medicaid/Chip Eligibility for Child Support Eligible Children*, Department of Health and Human Services, Office of the Assistant Secretary for Planning and Evaluation, ASPE Research Brief, July 2011, p. 5.

[95] Ibid., p. 12.

[96] See http://www.healthcarepayernews.com/print/14841, *CMS awards bonus payments to states for increasing CHIP enrollment*, December 19, 2012.)

[97] Kaiser Family Foundation, Focus on Health Reform, *Explaining Health Reform: Eligibility and Enrollment Processes For Medicaid, CHIP, and Subsidies in the Exchanges*, August 2010.

[98] Genevieve M. Kenney, Victoria Lynch, Allison Cook, and Samantha Phong, "Who And Where Are The Children Yet To Enroll In Medicaid And The Children's Health Insurance Program?," *Health Affairs* 29, no. 10 (2010): 1920– 1929, October 2010.

[99] Department of Health and Human Services, Administration for Children and Families, Office of Child Support Enforcement, Action Transmittal, AT-10-10, *State CSE Program Flexibility to Improve Interoperability with Medicaid and CHIP*, November 4, 2010.

[100] See the following webpage for state-by-state table showing the state "reasonable cost" definition— http://www.acf.hhs.gov/sites/default/files/programs/css/state_medical_support_contacts_and_program_information2.pdf. Based on the table, of the 21 states in which information was provided regarding the "reasonable cost" definition, 5 states have standards that exceed the 5% standard.

[101] Medicaid, CHIP, and the exchanges (beginning January 2014) also have "reasonable cost" standards.

[102] The Federal Consumer Credit Protection Act (15 USC §1673(b)(2)) limits garnishment to 50% of disposable earnings for a parent who owes child support who is the head of a household, and 60% for a person who owes child support who is not supporting a second family. These percentages increase by 5 percentage points, to 55% and 65% respectively, when the arrearages represent support that was due more than 12 weeks before the current pay period.

[103] The Kaiser Family Foundation and Health Research & Educational Trust, *Employer Health Benefits: 2012 Summary of Findings*, September 11, 2012.

[104] A quarter of the estimated 2012 premium for family coverage amounts to $1,079.

[105] As mentioned earlier, child support-eligible children are children age 18 or under living with only one biological parent.

[106] Department of Health and Human Services, Office of the Assistant Secretary for Planning and Evaluation, ASPE Research Brief, *Health Care Coverage and Medicaid/Chip Eligibility for Child Support Eligible Children*, by Stacey McMorrow, Genevieve Kenney, Allison Cook, and Christine Coyer (of the Urban Institute), July 2011, p. 5.

[107] The federal poverty level is $19,090 for a family of three in 2012. (There are separate higher poverty levels for Alaska and Hawaii.)

[108] The $880 figure equals 5% of gross income for a family of three living at the 2008 federal poverty level in the continental U.S.

[109] Based on 2012 data, a health plan contribution of $955 or more generally would be considered above "reasonable cost" (i.e., the 5% standard) for a mother with two children living in any state other than Alaska or Hawaii.

[110] *Federal Register* vol. 73, no. 140, Child Support Enforcement Program; Medical Support, July 21, 2008.

[111] Ibid., p. 42426.

[112] Pat Redmond (The Center on Budget and Policy Priorities), *A Medicaid Perspective on Medical Support Cooperation: A Study of Procedures in Five States*, The Kaiser Commission on Medicaid and the Uninsured, April 2005, p. 31.

[113] Genevieve Kenney, Allison Cook, and Lisa Dubay, *Progress Enrolling Children in Medicaid/CHIP: Who is Left and What are the Prospects for Covering More Children?*, Urban Institute and Robert Wood Johnson Foundation, December 2009.

[114] U.S. Congress, House Ways and Means Subcommittee on Oversight, *Hearing on Implementation of Tax Law Changes in the Affordable Care Act*, Written Testimony of Steven T. Miller (Deputy Commissioner for Services and Enforcement, Internal Revenue Service), September 11, 2012.

[115] CRS Report R41137, *Health Insurance Premium Credits in the Patient Protection and Affordable Care Act (ACA)*, by Bernadette Fernandez and Thomas Gabe, June 13, 2012, p. 15.

[116] Amy J. Davidoff, Bowen Garrett, Diane M. Makuc, and Matthew Schirmer, *Children Eligible for Medicaid but Not Enrolled: How Great a Policy Concern?*, , The Urban Institute, series A, no. A-41, September 2000, p. 6.

[117] Department of Health and Human Services, Administration for Children and Families, Office of Child Support Enforcement, *National Child Support Enforcement Strategic Plan for FY 2005-2009*, September 17, 2004.

[118] A federal open-ended match of 66% is available for state expenditures related to the costs of carrying out activities required under CSE program (i.e., Title IV-D of the Social Security Act).

[119] For example, Congress provided enhanced FFP to encourage paternity establishment and automation in the CSE program.

[120] P.L. 105-200 (the Child Support Performance and Incentive Act of 1998) established the Medical Child Support Working Group to study and provide recommendations on how to improve the enforcement of medical support obligations for children. It released its report, *21 Million Children's Health: Our Shared Responsibility*, in June 2000.

[121] The CSE incentive payment—which is based in part on five performance measures related to establishment of paternity and child support orders, collection of current and past-due child support payments, and cost-effectiveness— was statutorily set in P.L. 105-200. In the aggregate, incentive payments to states could not exceed $483 million for FY2008 (increased for inflation in years thereafter). Aggregate incentive payments to states totaled $513 million in FY2011 and $526 million in FY2012.

[122] Department of Health and Human Services, Administration for Children and Families, Office of Child Support Enforcement, *21 Million Children's Health: Our Shared Responsibility*, The Medical Child Support Working Group, June 2000.

[123] At the March 2-3, 1999 meeting, the Medical Child Support Working Group reviewed available data on medical support. Only seven states were able to provide data and some of those states had concerns about its validity. Census data was also reviewed and found to be unsatisfactory because it included information beyond the CSE program's caseload and the data could not be segregated by state. The Working Group agreed that a performance standard for medical support enforcement could not be set based on such limited and invalid data. (Source: Department of Health and Human Services, *Report to the Congress on Development of a Medical Support Incentive for the Child Support Enforcement Program*, June 23, 1999.)

[124] Under current federal law, states are accountable for providing reliable data on a timely basis or they receive no incentive payments. The data reliability provisions were enacted as part of P.L. 105-200, which established the current incentive payment system. They are in the law to ensure the integrity of the incentive payment system. The federal Office of Child Support Enforcement (OCSE) Office of Audit performs data reliability audits to evaluate the completeness, accuracy, security, and reliability of data reported and produced by state reporting systems. The audits help ensure that incentives under the Child Support Performance and Incentives Act of 1998 (P.L. 105-200) are earned and paid only on the basis of verifiable data and that the incentive payments system is fair and equitable. If an audit determines that a state's data are not complete and reliable for a given performance measure, the state receives zero payments for that measure. If states do not meet the data quality standards, they do not receive incentive payments and are subject to federal financial penalties.

[125] Department of Health and Human Services, Administration for Children and Families, Office of Child Support Enforcement, Action Transmittal, AT-11-10, *Notice of Changes to the OCSE-157 Form Regarding Medical Support*, October 17, 2011.

[126] Before FY2008, the federal government was required to match (at a 66% rate) incentive funds that states reinvested in the CSE program. P.L. 109-171 prohibited federal matching of incentive payments effective October 1, 2007 (i.e., FY2008). P.L. 111-5 temporarily reinstated federal matching of incentive payments for FY2009 and FY2010. There is currently no federal match on incentive payments.

[127] The previous 66% federal matching rate on incentive payments resulted in a near tripling of state CSE funding—in that for every dollar the state reinvested in the CSE program, the federal government matched that investment with about $2. Thereby, under old law, states were able to significantly leverage their investment through the federal financial structure.

[128] U.S. Census Bureau data indicate that in 2009 (latest available data) that of the 5.9 million custodial parents who were actually due child support payments in 2009, 41% received the full amount they were owed (from the noncustodial parent), 30% received partial payments, and 29% received no payments. Note: In 2009, an estimated 13.7 million parents had custody of 22.0 million children under age 21 while the other parent lived somewhere else. Of those custodial parents, 6.9 million had a child support order, but only 5.9 million custodial parents were actually due child support. Some of the reason why a custodial parent could have a child support order but not be due child support are: (1) their child or children are too old, (2) the noncustodial parent had died, or (3) the family lived together for part of the year before the survey interview. (Source: Timothy S. Grall, *Custodial Fathers and Mothers and Their Child Support: 2009*, U.S. Census Bureau, P60-240, December 2011, see Table 2, p. 6.)

[129] In FY2011, $144.6 billion in child support obligations ($33.3 billion in current support and $111.3 billion in past- due support) was owed to families receiving CSE services, but only $28.5 billion was paid ($20.8 billion current, $7.7 billion past-due).

[130] Western Interstate Child Support Enforcement Council (WiCSec), 29th Annual Training Conference, *Affordable Care Act and Child Support: Will There Be Medical Support After 2014?*, presented by Bob Williams, September 2012.

[131] Ibid.

[132] Stacey McMorrow, Genevieve M. Kenney, and Christine Coyer, *Addressing Barriers to Health Insurance Coverage Among Children: New Estimates for the Nation, California, New York, and Texas*, The Urban Institute, May 2012.

[133] Note that low-income individuals in states that do not expand Medicaid are exempt from the individual health coverage mandate.

[134] In some cases, health insurance coverage is not an issue because it is already being provided by the other parent.

[135] *Congressional Record*, Senate, Remarks by Russell B. Long, March 14, 1972, p. 8291.

[136] In FY2011, families receiving TANF cash benefits comprised 13% of the CSE caseload.

[137] Barbara Wolfe, *Poverty and Poor Health: Can Health Care Reform Narrow the Rich-Poor Gap?*, University of Wisconsin-Madison, June 2011, p. 29.

[138] The other two goals are to provide more security and stability to those who have health insurance and to slow the growth of health care costs. Source: Jennifer Burnszynski, *Child Support Report, vol. 32, no. 1*, "Medical Child Support and Health Reform: New Opportunities, New Questions," Department of Health and Human Services, Administration for Children and Families, Office of Child Support Enforcement, January 2010, pp. 1-2.

[139] National Conference of State Legislatures, *Child Support Administration*, updated 2012.

[140] Lisa Dubay and Genevieve Kenney, "Addressing Coverage Gaps For Low-Income Parents," *Health Affairs*, vol. 23 no. 2, March 2004, pp. 225-234. See also: Kaiser Commission on Medicaid and the Uninsured, *Expanding Health Coverage for Low-Income Adults: Filling the Gaps in Medicaid Eligibility*, May 2009.

[141] Vicki Turetsky, *Child Support Report, April 2012*, "Commissioner's Voice—Interoperable computer systems will mean better customer service," Department of Health and Human Services, Administration for Children and Families, Office of Child Support Enforcement.

[142] Massachusetts Administrative Office of the Trial Court, Trial Court Information Services, Testimony of Craig D. Burlingame (Chief Information Officer) before the House Ways and Means Subcommittee on Human Resources at hearing on No-Cost Improvements to Child Support Enforcement, March 20, 2012.

[143] Vicki Turetsky, *Child Support Report, April 2012*, "Commissioner's Voice—Interoperable computer systems will mean better customer service," Department of Health and Human Services, Administration for Children and Families, Office of Child Support Enforcement.

[144] Ibid.

[145] Department of Health and Human Services, Administration for Children and Families, Office of Child Support Enforcement, Commissioner's Voice, *Interoperable computer systems will mean better customer service*, April 5, 2012.

[146] Cari DeSantis and Sarah Fass Hiatt, *Data Sharing in Public Benefit Programs: An Action Agenda for Removing Barriers*, Coalition for Access and Opportunity, November 2012, p. 4.

[147] Philip F. Cooper and Ayah E. Johnson, *Employment-related health insurance in 1987*, April 1993.

[148] *Federal Register*, vol. 50, no. 200; Department of Health and Human Services, Administration for Children and Families, Office of Child Support Enforcement, *Child Support Enforcement Program: Medical Support Enforcement, Final Rule*, October 16, 1985, pp. 41887-41895.

[149] *Federal Register*, vol. 53, no. 180; Department of Health and Human Services, Administration for Children and Families, Office of Child Support Enforcement, *Child Support Enforcement Program: Medical Support Enforcement, Final Rule*, September 16, 1988, pp. 30614-30622.

[150] Department of Health and Human Services, Administration for Children and Families, Office of Child Support Enforcement, Dear Colleague Letter, DCL-93-12, *HCFA Final Rule-Poverty Level Pregnant Women Eligible for Medicaid*, February 23, 1993.

[151] See http://www.acf.hhs.gov/programs/css/resource/medical-support-for-federal-agencies.

[152] Ibid.

[153] *Federal Register*, vol. 73, no. 140; Department of Health and Human Services, Administration for Children and Families, Office of Child Support Enforcement, *Medical Support: Final Regulation*, July 21, 2008, pp. 42416-42442.

[154] Department of Health and Human Services, Administration for Children and Families, Office of Child Support Enforcement, *FY2009 Annual Report to Congress*, December 2011. See also Department of Health and Human Services, Administration for Children and Families, Office of Child Support Enforcement, *FY2010 Preliminary Report*, May 2011. Also see Department of Health and Human Services, Administration for Children and Families, Office of Child Support Enforcement, *FY2011 Preliminary Report*, October 2012.

[155] OCSE defines a CSE "case" as a noncustodial parent (mother, father, or putative/alleged father) who is now or eventually may be obligated under law for the support of a child or children receiving services under the CSE program. If the noncustodial parent owes support for two children by different women, that would be considered two cases; if both children have the same mother, that would be considered one case.

[156] In FY2001, medical support orders that stipulated the provision of health insurance coverage applied to 49% of *all CSE cases with a child support order established*, and as mentioned above 93% of *cases with a medical support order*. Health insurance coverage was provided as ordered in 31% of those cases.

In: Child Support Issues
Editor: Rene Pellerin

ISBN: 978-1-62808-376-7

Chapter 2

CHILD SUPPORT ENFORCEMENT: INCARCERATION AS THE LAST RESORT PENALTY FOR NONPAYMENT OF SUPPORT*

Carmen Solomon-Fears, Alison M. Smith and Carla Berry

SUMMARY

The Child Support Enforcement (CSE) program was signed into law in 1975 (P.L. 93-647) as a federal-state program to enhance the well-being of families by making child support a reliable source of income. The CSE program is based on the premise that both parents are financially responsible for their children. The CSE program is operated in all 50 states, the District of Columbia, Guam, Puerto Rico, and the U.S. Virgin Islands, and by several Indian tribes or tribal organizations. State CSE programs have at their disposal a wide variety of methods by which to obtain child support obligations. In addition, states under their own authority and the authority of their courts can use the threat of incarceration and/or actual incarceration.

Nonpayment of support may subject a noncustodial parent to criminal sanctions in three situations: (1) a finding of contempt of court for failure to obey a court's child support order, (2) prosecution under a

* This is an edited, reformatted and augmented version of a Congressional Research Service publication, CRS Report for Congress R42389, prepared for Members and Committees of Congress, from www.crs.gov, dated March 6, 2012.

state criminal nonsupport statute, or (3) prosecution under federal criminal penalties for nonpayment of child support. Contempt of court is classified as either "civil" or "criminal." Civil contempt occurs when an individual willfully disobeys a court order or rule. Criminal contempt occurs when an individual interferes with the ability of the court to function properly. Judges can sentence individuals to imprisonment upon a finding of contempt.

Many contend that the incarceration of persons for nonpayment of child support is both wrong and counterproductive. They say that criminalizing nonpayment of child support by making it a misdemeanor and/or felony disproportionately affects low-income noncustodial parents who more likely than not are just as poor or poorer than the mother and children owed child support payments. They assert that incarceration means that the noncustodial parent is not working and earning money and that having a criminal record lowers a person's job prospects. They also contend that the negative ramifications of being in jail include a weakened bond between the noncustodial parent and his or her children and family and a high probability that the individual will ultimately be re-incarcerated for nonpayment of child support or other infractions or crimes.

Others say that for some noncustodial parents, the threat of being incarcerated for nonpayment of support is not enough. For these persons, they say that incarceration is necessary. They contend that some noncustodial parents would rather quit their jobs, go from job to job, work in the underground economy (where earnings are not reported to anyone), or engage in illegal activity rather than meet their child support obligations. They argue that child support is a source of income that could mean the difference between poverty and self-sufficiency for some families. They say that children ought not to be short-changed because of recalcitrant noncustodial parents, and maintain that nonpayment of child support is a real crime and should be treated as such.

Using jail as an option for nonpayment of child support has many implications: Are low-income noncustodial parents who are unable to fulfill their child support obligations penalized for being poor? Should noncustodial parents charged with civil contempt of court be entitled to an attorney? Should noncustodial parents whose only offense is nonpayment of child support be incarcerated in settings known to be violent and dangerous? Should incarcerating noncustodial parents be eliminated as an option due to the high costs associated with incarceration? This report includes an Appendix that indicates that all 50 states and the District of Columbia have criminal penalties for nonpayment of child support. Table A-1 shows state statute citations and the maximum penalties associated with nonpayment of child support.

INTRODUCTION

Child support is the cash payment that noncustodial parents are obligated to pay for the financial support of their children. Child support payments enable parents who do not live with their children to fulfill their financial responsibility to their children by contributing to the payment of childrearing costs.

The Child Support Enforcement (CSE) program was signed into law in 1975 (P.L. 93-647, Title IV-D of the Social Security Act) as a federal-state program to help strengthen families by securing financial support for children from their noncustodial parent on a consistent and continuing basis and by helping some families to remain self-sufficient and off public assistance. The CSE program is based on the premise that both parents are financially responsible for their children. Basic responsibility for administering the CSE program is left to the states, but the federal government has a major role in dictating the major design features of state programs; funding, monitoring, and evaluating state programs; providing technical assistance; and giving states help in locating noncustodial parents and obtaining child support payments. Congress, through legislative changes, has broadened the mission of the CSE program. The CSE program has evolved over time from a "welfare cost-recovery" program into a "family-first" service delivery program that seeks to enhance the well-being of families by making child support a reliable source of income.[1]

Included in their available methods to collect child support obligations, states use the threat of jail and actual incarceration in jail.[2] Many states bring charges of civil or criminal contempt of court or criminal nonsupport against noncustodial parents who fail to pay child support.

All states have criminal statutes that relate to the failure to pay child support. Thus, in all states, failure to pay child support is technically a crime under the state's criminal nonsupport statutes. However, many states choose to treat failure to pay child support less harshly by treating it as a violation of a court order. A violation of a court order is usually referred to as contempt of court and, depending on the state, it may be considered a civil offense, a criminal offense, or both.

In the CSE program, although a general protocol is usually followed, the individual caseworker has discretion over how to manage a case. For example, the caseworker determines which child support collection methods to use. After the CSE caseworker determines that he or she has spent an appropriate amount of time trying to get a noncustodial parent to meet his or her child support obligation, the worker often has the authority to have a warrant issued to bring the noncompliant noncustodial parent before a judge. Some noncustodial parents contend that they appeared in court in compliance to a subpoena and then were immediately arrested and put in jail after the court hearing.

The task of trying to persuade noncustodial parents to pay their child support obligation is an ongoing and, at times, futile duty for many judges. The threat of jail—or actual incarceration— for failure to pay child support is widely acknowledged to be just a temporary fix, but many judges contend that it is their most productive leverage in child support cases. Given that about 70% of child support arrearages (i.e., past due child support) are owed by noncustodial parents with no reported income or income of $10,000 or less per year, the inability of low-income noncustodial parents to pay child support will likely be a constant and ongoing problem.[3]

National data do not exist with respect to how often the incarceration option is used.[4] So, if incarceration of noncustodial parents for nonpayment of child support is viewed as an issue, there are no data to reflect the magnitude of the problem.

BACKGROUND

The CSE program is operated in all 50 states, the District of Columbia, Guam, Puerto Rico, and the U.S. Virgin Islands, and by several Indian tribes or tribal organizations. The CSE program provides seven major services on behalf of children: (1) parent location, (2) paternity establishment, (3) establishment of child support orders, (4) review and modification of child support orders, (5) collection of child support payments, (6) distribution of child support payments, and (7) establishment and enforcement of medical support.

The CSE program has at its disposal a wide variety of methods by which to obtain child support obligations. Collection methods used by state CSE agencies include

- income withholding,
- intercept of federal and state income tax refunds,
- intercept of unemployment compensation,
- liens against property,

- reporting child support obligations to credit bureaus,
- intercept of lottery winnings,
- sending insurance settlement information to CSE agencies,
- authority to withhold or suspend driver's licenses, professional licenses, and recreational and sporting licenses of persons who owe past-due support,[5]
- authority to seize assets of debtor parents held by public or private retirement funds and financial institutions, and
- authority for the Secretary of State to deny, revoke, or restrict passports of debtor parents.

In addition, federal CSE law requires states to enact and implement the Uniform Interstate Family Support Act (UIFSA) and expand full faith and credit procedures[6] (so as to effectively enforce interstate child support cases). Federal law also provides for international enforcement of child support. In addition, federal criminal penalties may be imposed in certain cases.[7] Moreover, all jurisdictions also have civil or criminal contempt-of-court procedures and criminal nonsupport laws (see the *Appendix*). This option means that it is possible for all states and jurisdictions to incarcerate certain noncustodial parents who owe past-due child support.

The most effective child support enforcement tool is income withholding, a procedure by which automatic deductions are made from wages or other income. Once initiated, income withholding can keep child support flowing to the family on a regular basis. In FY2010, about 67% of the $32 billion collected by the states for child support payments was obtained through income withholding, 6% from the unemployment intercept offset, 6% by way of the federal income tax refund offset, 4% from other states, less than 1% from the state income tax refund offset, and 16% ($5 billion) from other sources.[8] Sporadic data from the federal Office of Child Support Enforcement (OCSE) indicate that roughly $3.5 billion of the $5 billion amount from other sources is from child support collected through banks, credit unions, and other financial institutions pursuant to the financial institution data match program; and perhaps about $1 billion (per year) is from collections obtained due to the driver's license suspension program.[9] Based on these rough estimates, probably less than 2% of child support collections can be associated with the threat of incarceration. If a noncustodial parent is actually incarcerated because of nonpayment of child support, the likelihood of receipt of child support payments from that parent during the period of incarceration is very small.

It should be noted that even before the enactment of the CSE program in 1975, states individually and collectively tried to address the problem of nonpayment of child support. For example, in 1910 the National Conference of Commissioners on Uniform State Laws approved the Uniform Desertion and Non-Support Act, which imposed criminal penalties on fathers who failed to support their children. The 1910 act sought to improve the enforcement of the duties of support, but it did not take into account husbands and fathers who fled the jurisdiction.[10] As the U.S. population became more mobile and noncustodial parents and their children increasingly lived in different states, welfare agencies had to support some destitute families because the extradition process was inefficient and often unsuccessful. In 1950, The National Conference of Commissions on Uniform State Laws published the Uniform Reciprocal Enforcement of Support Act (URESA). The commission stated that, "The purposes of this act are to improve and extend by reciprocal legislation the enforcement of duties of support and to make uniform the law with respect thereto." URESA sought to enforce the provisions in two ways: criminal enforcement and civil enforcement.[11]

Although jail has been a method to enforce child support obligations for a long time, from the outset many acknowledged that it was counterproductive to put the noncustodial parent in jail. Commentary on the 1950 version of URESA indicated the following:

> Everyone was agreed that the return of the obligor to face criminal charges in the state from which he had fled was of limited value. If convicted, he would be put in jail and the state would still have the burden of support of the destitute family. Even when free again, he would be under the heavy handicap of "a man with a criminal record" in finding a job and supporting his family. However, the commissioners finally decided to leave criminal enforcement in the Act because it was the traditional method of solving the problem and it was not certain that civil enforcement would take care of all cases; and it was felt that, while actual extradition would be of little use, the threat of extradition might be a powerful weapon in the case of shiftless and slippery obligors.[12]

State and federal laws and procedures that penalize noncustodial parents for not paying child support by "locking them up" have gained sympathy in recent years from a wide range of interested parties. Child support experts and state policymakers now generally categorize noncustodial parents who do not consistently pay their child support obligation on a timely basis as "can't pay" and "won't pay" parents.[13] While policymakers and the public are somewhat sympathetic to those who cannot pay, they are angry with those that will not pay. In response, states and the federal government have developed and implemented aggressive child enforcement tools to pursue “won't pay” parents who refuse to meet their child support obligation despite having the financial resources to do so. The increasingly common use of criminal statutes and contempt of court orders in child support cases reflects society’s growing frustration with “won't pay” parents.[14] (It should be noted that although this either-or delineation may at first seem straightforward, in practice it can be very complicated and many low-income noncustodial parents claim that they are mistakenly lumped into the “won’t pay” group when in reality they do not have the income or resources to pay.)

Other countries also use the jail option. For example, in England and Wales if a nonresident parent refuses to pay the child maintenance he or she owes, the Child Support Agency can apply to the courts for a warrant of commitment. This warrant can legally send a nonresident parent to prison for up to six weeks.[15] Moreover, as in the United States, even if the nonresident parent is sent to prison, he or she is still obligated to pay all of the child support owed. Among the 14 countries studied in a 2009 report, 3 did not imprison persons for failure to pay child support arrears.[16] Two of the three countries that did not imprison were Australia and Finland. In addition, the report noted that although Denmark specifies criminal prosecution and imprisonment in various documents, it has never in practice prosecuted or incarcerated anyone because of nonpayment of child support.[17]

As mentioned above, one of the services provided by the CSE program is review and modification of child support orders. A prevalent viewpoint holds that an effective modification process can help assure that child support orders remain appropriate and prevent the accumulation of inappropriate child support debt.

The section below discusses ways in which the nonpayment of child support can result in a noncustodial parent being incarcerated. Laws concerning most child support enforcement activities are civil, but nonpayment of child support may subject a noncustodial parent to criminal sanctions in three situations: (1) a finding of contempt of court for failure to obey a court’s child support order—contempt of court is classified as either criminal or civil; (2) prosecution under a state criminal nonsupport statute; or (3) prosecution under the Child Support Recovery Act of 1992, as amended in 1998 (P.L. 102-521 and P.L. 105-187).[18] Anecdotally, it appears that it is not uncommon for low-income noncustodial parents to be incarcerated for nonpayment of child support or contempt of court charges that relate to nonpayment of child support.[19] Unfortunately, national data do not exist with respect to how often the incarceration option is used. CSE agencies generally do not track arrests for nonpayment of child support and the record-keeping of sheriffs' offices or prosecuting attorneys' offices on this topic is sporadic, nonexistent, and/or inconsistent across jurisdictions.[20]

Contempt of Court

Contempt of court is a legal term that means that the individual in question is not following a court order. State courts have the authority to punish individuals for violating their valid judgments or decrees. Certain acts or omissions that embarrass the court, lessen its authority or dignity, or obstruct the administration of justice constitute contempt. A judge who feels someone is improperly challenging or ignoring the court's authority has the power to declare the defiant person in contempt of court. Contempt is classified as either civil or criminal.[21]

If the purpose of the penalty imposed is for the benefit of a private party to the action, the contempt is generally classified as civil.[22] Civil contempt occurs when an individual willfully disobeys a court order or rule. This is sometimes referred to as indirect contempt because it occurs outside the judge's immediate realm and evidence must be presented to the judge to prove the contempt.[23] An individual who is found to be in civil contempt of court may be fined, jailed, or both as a consequence of his or her actions. The fine or jailing is meant to coerce the individual into obeying the court, not to punish the person, and the person is to be released from jail just as soon as he or she complies with the court order.[24] In family or domestic relations law, civil contempt is one way a court enforces child support orders that have been violated. In fact, parties seeking payment of child support often ask courts, through motions for civil contempt, to send the defendant (i.e., the noncustodial parent) to jail unless he or she comes up with the money owed.[25] In a civil contempt of court case, the individual is no longer in contempt (and thereby free) once he or she complies with the court's requirements (e.g., fully pay all child support arrearages, make timely child support payments in accordance with a court-sanctioned agreement, or participate in a work and/or training program so as to be able to make child support payments at a later date).

However, if the purpose of the penalty is to vindicate the authority of the court, the contempt is classified as criminal.[26] Criminal contempt occurs when an individual interferes with the ability of the court to function properly. For example, if an individual yells at the judge or jury, it could be considered criminal contempt of court. An individual who is found to be in criminal contempt of court may be fined, jailed, or both as punishment for his or her actions. Criminal contempt of court charges are punitive, in that their intent is to deter future acts of contempt by punishing the offender no matter what happens in the underlying proceeding. In other words, criminal contempt of court charges become separate charges from the underlying case. Unlike civil contempt sanctions, criminal contempt charges may live on after resolution of the underlying case.[27]

Although contempt of court proceedings are generally classified as either civil or criminal, it is generally agreed that it is often hard to determine how a particular act or infraction should be properly classified.[28] Interested parties also agree that judges should more carefully determine whether to impose civil or criminal contempt of court rulings. This is because "an incorrect decision (wrongly classifying the contempt proceeding as civil) can increase the risk of wrongful incarceration by depriving the defendant of the procedural protections (including counsel) that the Constitution would demand in a criminal proceeding."[29]

Civil Contempt of Court

According to CSE documents, civil contempt actions are generally brought against noncustodial parents who have very poor child support payment histories, are unemployed or self-employed, or have no regular income that can be withheld through income withholding.[30] The basic purpose of a civil contempt action is to encourage compliance with the child support order.[31] In fact, in general, a finding of current ability to pay is a prerequisite to a civil contempt ruling.[32] In a civil contempt action, the purpose is to force compliance by the noncustodial parent.[33] The sanction usually falls into three categories: (1) coercive/punitive fines (paid to the court), (2) compensatory/ remedial fines (paid to the custodial parent), and (3) incarceration.[34] However, any fine or imprisonment is generally considered improper unless it benefits the custodial parent and the children and allows the noncustodial parent to purge himself or herself (i.e., avoid punishment) by complying with clearly stated and attainable requirements.[35]

According to arguments made during the *Turner v. Rogers* Supreme Court case, "A court may not impose punishment in a civil contempt proceeding when it is clearly established that the alleged contemnor is unable to comply with the terms of the order. And once a noncustodial parent who is delinquent in paying his or her child support obligation complies with the underlying order, he is purged of the contempt and is free."[36] Some commentators characterize this situation by saying that "He carries the keys of his prison in his own pockets."[37] The Court has made clear (in a case not involving the right to counsel) that, where civil contempt is at issue, the Fourteenth Amendment's Due Process Clause allows a state to provide fewer procedural protections than in a criminal case.[38] Further, a state may place the burden of proving inability to pay on the defendant.[39]

Some commentators assert that although the intent may be that persons who are unable to comply with court requirements because they do not have the money to pay child support obligations should not be charged with contempt of court, in practice this may occur because some noncustodial parents are mistakenly thought to be able to pay and many noncustodial parents cannot prove that they are not able to pay.

Criminal Contempt of Court

A strictly penal sanction is supposed to be imposed only in cases wherein the defendant is provided essential due process protections. These due process protections include the right to notice of the offense, the right to present a defense, the right to call witnesses, an impartial judge, and, in some jurisdictions, the right to counsel and a trial by jury.[40]

A criminal contempt proceeding is considerably more complicated than a civil contempt proceeding. Initiation of the proceeding may require a more formal notice than is provided the civil defendant in the motion and order to show cause, although a formal indictment is not necessary.[41] The possibility of an indigency hearing, a jury trial, and a change of judge potentially makes the process a very long one.[42]

Nonetheless, there are occasions when criminal contempt may be effective. In cases where a noncustodial parent has been charged with civil contempt on several occasions but never voluntarily makes child support payments until the jail term is imminent, a criminal contempt action may change his or her attitude about compliance. In addition, a court may set consecutive jail terms for multiple contempt of court rulings. Moreover, criminal contempt might be the only available remedy to punish a noncustodial parent who willingly limited his or her ability to pay child support (out of spite) by quitting a job or taking one at a much lower salary.[43]

Supreme Court Case—Representation in Civil Cases

Parents can be jailed without a trial because failure to pay child support is usually handled as a civil matter—contempt of court. This means that if the noncustodial parent is found guilty of contempt of court and ordered to appear at a hearing, he or she can be sent to jail unless willing and able to satisfy the child support obligation. As mentioned, these civil defendants generally are not entitled to the constitutional protections that criminal defendants receive, including the presumption of innocence or the right to an attorney.

In contrast, indigent criminal defendants have a right to court-appointed attorneys, who typically are paid with tax dollars. Recently, the U.S. Supreme Court was asked to determine whether the Fourteenth Amendment's Due Process Clause requires a state to provide legal representation to an indigent noncustodial parent who is subject to a child support order and faces imprisonment due to noncompliance with that order.

In *Turner v. Rogers*,[44] the Court declined to rule that due process requires legal representation in such instances where other procedural safeguards exist. These safeguards center around a defendant's ability to pay and include

> (1) notice to the defendant that his ability to pay is a critical issue in the contempt proceeding; (2) the use of a form (or the equivalent) to elicit relevant financial information; (3) an opportunity at the hearing for the defendant to respond to statements and questions about his financial status; and (4) an express finding by the court that the defendant has the ability to pay.[45]

The case at issue was a South Carolina child support case wherein the defendant, Michael Turner, spent a year in jail for failure to pay back child support after a hearing conducted without legal representation. He presented some evidence of his inability to work, but the court made no finding as to the defendant's indigent status or ability to pay. He was not convicted of a crime; the year in jail was not a punishment, per se. Turner was being held in contempt of court, and the jail time was a means to induce the payment of nearly $6,000 in past-due child support.[46]

In reaching its decision, the Court relied on factors set forth in *Mathews v. Eldridge*,[47] to determine what safeguards are required to make a civil proceeding fundamentally fair. Specially, the Court stated

> A requirement that the State provide counsel to the noncustodial parent in these cases could create an asymmetry of representation that would "alter significantly the nature of the proceeding.... Doing so could

> mean a degree of formality or delay that would unduly slow payment to those immediately in need. And, perhaps more important for present purposes, doing so could make the proceedings less fair overall, increasing the risk of a decision that would erroneously deprive a family of the support it is entitled to receive. The needs of such families play an important role in our analysis."[48]

The Court determined that the straightforward nature of child support proceedings, the lack of representation by the custodial parent, and the existence of other procedural safeguards outside of legal representation all suggested that the Due Process Clause did not mandate appointment of an attorney under the circumstances presented. However, the Court found that the lower court violated Turner's rights by not ensuring that he had counsel or other procedural safeguards to provide notice that his ability to pay was a critical issue or a form to elicit financial information to make such a determination.[49] It is important to note that this decision did not address instances where the child support is owed to the state (i.e., reimbursement of welfare funds) or where complex matters are presented.[50]

During discussion, debate, and arguments concerning the *Turner v. Rogers* case, the concept of whether nonpaying noncustodial parents should be viewed as deadbeats versus turnips[51] was a recurring point of contention.[52] Those who likened noncustodial parents with high child support arrearages to deadbeats argued that some defendants, most often fathers, somehow develop a belief that their financial and emotional obligations to their children ended when their relationship with the children's mother did. These observers also claimed that other noncustodial parents withhold child support in order to punish or control their ex-spouses. They asserted that for these two groups of defendants, sometimes the threat of jail, followed up by actual jail time (so as not to make the threat an empty one), is the only way to get such noncustodial parents to comply with their child support obligations.

Those who likened certain noncustodial parents to turnips claimed that many low-income child support defendants were turnips from whom no one—not the custodial parent, not the CSE caseworkers, not the judge—could squeeze one penny. They asserted that the majority of low-income noncustodial parents who end up in jail are turnips, low-income defendants who cannot afford to purge themselves of contempt. According to several analysts and Turner's legal team, the turnips of the world are those who most often end up in jail, which both needlessly deprives them of freedom (and the ability to find a job) and fails to achieve the state's goal of inspiring compliance with child support.[53]

Because the defendant "holds the keys to his own jail cell" in a civil contempt case, with the ability to end the jail time by complying with the order, it has historically been considered differently than a jail sentence of a specified term for criminal contempt.

According to Turner, the problem was that he just did not have the money to pay. Further, because he did not have a lawyer at his contempt hearing, he was unable to prove it. Because he was sent to jail to force him to comply with a debt he could not pay, he likened his situation to debtors' prison. The mother of his children and her supporters, including the two U.S. Senators from South Carolina, argued that granting civil contempt defendants the right to counsel would actually lead to inequality in the justice system for custodial parents, who do not have such a right.[54] Under prior U.S. Supreme Court rulings, indigent criminal defendants have a right to court-appointed attorneys, who typically are paid with tax dollars. But the Supreme Court has declined to grant similar rights in civil proceedings that could result in jail time and declined to do so again in *Turner*. However, the U.S. Supreme Court did find that the state court violated the defendant's constitutional rights by sentencing him to imprisonment without first determining whether he had the ability to pay.[55] Thus, the Court set aside a unanimous ruling by the South Carolina Supreme Court[56] and sent the case back to the lower court for "further proceedings not inconsistent with this opinion."[57]

Criminal Nonsupport

In many instances, CSE actions are not successful in collecting past-due child support. In those cases, the CSE caseworker via an attorney may pursue criminal charges against the delinquent obligor. There are criminal offenses for nonsupport of children at both the state and federal level.

State Actions

All 50 states and the District of Columbia have state-specific or jurisdiction-specific criminal statutes that relate to the failure to pay support in purely intrastate or intra-jurisdiction cases. In some of these states (including DC), the attorneys who establish and enforce child support obligations in civil court have the discretion to file criminal charges against a noncustodial parent.[58] Other states have a referral process where the child support attorney refers the case to the district attorney or prosecutor to review for criminal prosecution. Also, some states appoint child support attorneys as special prosecutors solely for the purpose of bringing an action under the state criminal nonsupport statute.[59] Although CSE program remedies such as income withholding and income tax refund intercept are still the most often used enforcement tools, criminal nonsupport proceedings can be a useful deterrent to noncompliance. In most states, the usual procedure is for all available civil remedies to be exhausted before resorting to the use of criminal nonsupport. It can be argued that where CSE remedies have proven unsuccessful or where the noncustodial parent has been evading civil remedies, a criminal charge can be effective in bringing about payment. In most states, the normal rules of evidence apply to a criminal nonsupport action. Depending on local practice, the action is initiated by filing a criminal complaint or indictment. Based on the initial finding, a judge may issue a warrant or summons. Like other state criminal actions, the initial pleading must allege all elements of the crime in such a manner that allows the defendant to understand the charge and prepare a defense. State law defines the elements of the crime. The standard of proof in these cases is proof beyond a reasonable doubt. See *Table A-1* in the *Appendix* for a state-by-state listing of criminal nonpayment of child support statutes.

Federal Criminal Penalties

During the early 1990s, research revealed that a significant number of noncustodial parents were able to meet their child support obligations but intentionally chose not to do so. The chances of successfully escaping one's child support duties increased substantially when the noncustodial parent crossed state lines so as not to pay child support. The Child Support Recovery Act of 1992 (P.L. 102-521) addressed the problem of interstate enforcement of child support by taking the incentive out of moving to another state to avoid paying child support. According to the congressional report on the legislation, "The bill is designed to target interstate cases only. These are the cases which state officials report to be clearly the most difficult to enforce, especially the 'hard core' group of parents who flagrantly refuse to pay and whom traditional extradition procedures have utterly failed to bring to justice."[60]

P.L. 102-521 imposed a federal criminal penalty for the willful failure to pay a past due child support obligation to a child who resides in another state that has remained unpaid for longer than a year or is greater than $5,000. For the first conviction, the penalty is a fine of up to $5,000, imprisonment for not more than six months, or both; for a second conviction, the penalty is a fine of not more than $250,000, imprisonment for up to two years, or both.[61] This federal criminal penalty was seen as an additional child support enforcement tool or remedy to be used for especially difficult cases in which state-level options had been exhausted and the noncustodial parent with the ability to pay seemed to be intent on evading his or her child support obligations.[62]

After the 1992 law was implemented, there was concern that by providing for a maximum punishment of just six months in prison for a first offense, even very egregious cases of nonsupport were only considered misdemeanors.[63] In response to assertions that the 1992 law did not adequately address more serious instances of nonpayment of child support obligations, Congress passed the Deadbeat Parents Punishment Act of 1998 (P.L. 105-187). The law establishes two new categories of felony offenses, subject to a two-year maximum prison term. The offenses are (1) traveling in interstate or foreign commerce with the intent to evade a support obligation if the obligation has remained unpaid for more than one year or is greater than $5,000; and (2) willfully failing to pay a child support obligation regarding a child residing in another state if the obligation has remained unpaid for more than two years or is greater than $10,000.[64]

"Project Save Our Children" is the mechanism through which the federal criminal penalties for nonsupport law is carried out. The Project Save Our Children initiative is conducted by officials from the HHS Office of Inspector General, the OCSE, the Department of Justice, state CSE agencies, and local law enforcement organizations working together to pursue chronic delinquent parents who owe large sums of child support. Its goal is to increase child support collections through the identification, investigation, and, when warranted, prosecutions of flagrant, delinquent child support offenders.

According to HHS, in FY2006 Project Save Our Children, received over 10,000 cases from the states. As a result of the work of the task forces, in FY2006 986 arrests were made nationwide and 872 individuals were sentenced. Federal investigations resulted in a total of $39.6 million in restitution being ordered with $35.8 million actually collected in FY2006.[65] In FY2007, the Project Save Our Children program resulted in about $8.1 million in child support collections from 1,139 child support cases.[66]

IMPLICATIONS

Many policymakers argue that the threat of jail usually brings noncustodial parents who are employed or have access to income or assets into compliance with child support orders. In contrast, low-income noncustodial parents who do not have the money to pay their child support obligation go directly to jail (because they are unable to comply before the threat is actualized due to their lack of funds).[67]

The threat of jailing noncustodial parents who are delinquent in meeting their child support obligations is intended to coerce them to pay, but if they have no money, they cannot pay. Moreover, in many instances these noncustodial parents have used up their goodwill with relatives and friends and thus can no longer borrow from others to meet their obligations. Thus, in the case of some low-income noncustodial parents, jail becomes their reality because they do not have the income or assets to eliminate the threat.

According to many analysts, the threat of jail may be a good public policy tool, but actually making good on the threat generally is not productive. In other words, putting low-income noncustodial parents in jail, especially when it is known that they are unemployed and without the means to pay their child support obligations, does not seem to be effective in gaining financial or emotional help for children. But, observers ask, how can use of a threat be effective if everyone knows that there are no teeth behind it?

Many noncustodial fathers maintain that the CSE system is dismissive of their financial condition and continues to pursue child support payments (current as well as arrearages) even when it knows that many of them can barely support themselves. They argue that for welfare families, the CSE program generally does not improve their child's well-being because their child support payments are used to benefit the state and federal government (i.e., welfare reimbursement) rather than their child. They contend that the CSE program causes conflicts between them and their child's mother because the women often use it as leverage by threatening to report them to CSE authorities, take them back to court, have more of their wages garnished, or have them arrested.[68]

Some commentators assert that jails are expensive, dangerous places in which people become aggressive in order to manage their fears or survive the sentence. Therefore, they contend that although most of these people may have been nonviolent before they were incarcerated, they often are no longer so after being in jail or prison.[69]

Noncustodial parents who are incarcerated for violations related to nonpayment of child support are usually put in jail rather than prison.[70] One widely held myth is that jails only hold nonviolent offenders. To the contrary, jails receive individuals pending arraignment and hold those awaiting trial, conviction, or sentencing. They also hold probation, parole, and bail-bond violators. Some of these individuals are violent persons.

It is generally agreed that violence is a part of prison life. It has been noted that the lack of outrage over prison violence is testament to the fact that it is considered a normal and acceptable part of behavior inside prison.[71] According to one report: "The rates of physical assault for male inmates is over 18 times higher than assault victimization rates for males in the general population, and rates for female inmates are over 27 times higher than their nonincarcerated counterparts."[72] Thus, many observers both inside and outside the criminal justice system concede that jails and prisons should primarily be used for violent offenders and that less harsh alternatives should be used for non-violent offenders such as those whose only offense is nonpayment of child support.[73]

According to a report by the American Civil Liberties Union (ACLU), "Incarceration has a devastating effect on men and women whose only remaining crime is that they are poor." Although the report pertains to legal financial obligations (i.e., fines and/or costs imposed on the defendant by a court), the following commentary could also apply to low-income noncustodial parents who are unable to handle their child support obligations.

> Upon release, they face the daunting prospect of having to rebuild their lives yet again. Even for those men and women with unpaid LFOs [Legal Financial Obligations] who do not end up back behind bars, their substantial legal debts pose a significant, and at times insurmountable, barrier as they attempt to re-enter society. They see their incomes reduced, their credit ratings worsen, their prospects for housing and employment dim, and their chances of ending up back in jail or prison increase. Many must make hard choices each month as they attempt to balance their needs and those of their families with their LFOs. They also remain tethered to the criminal justice system—sometimes decades after they complete their sentences—and live under constant threat of being sent back to jail or prison, solely because they cannot pay what has become an unmanageable legal debt.[74]

Some commentators note that jail generally increases a person's stress and negatively impacts his or her emotional/mental and physical health.[75] They claim that some inmates adopt an aggressive persona out of self-preservation (because the inmate believes that it's a matter of intimidate or be intimidated). They also contend that many persons self-medicate (i.e., use legal or illegal drugs) both inside and outside of jail/prison to counteract the negative impacts, which often results in further repercussions that usually negatively affect the building of positive, strong parent-child relationships and sometimes result in recidivism.[76] Many observers maintain that putting nonviolent persons in jail is often counterproductive especially in times of tight state and local budgets and/or when jail/prison overcrowding is an issue.

The United States incarcerates more individuals than any other nation.[77] In 2008, the Pew Center on the States reported that 1 in every 100 adults in the United States now lives behind bars. According to MDRC, a nonpartisan research organization, "Corrections costs exceed $65 billion per year, with most of the total borne by state and local governments."[78] To save costs and to increase the effectiveness and efficiency of the criminal justice system, many states and localities are making use of community service (i.e., unpaid community work), halfway houses, electronic monitoring, court supervision, and community sentencing as alternatives to incarcerating people in jail or prison.

Many policy analysts contend that the incarceration of persons for nonviolent offenses, such as nonpayment of child support, is both wrong and counterproductive.[79] They say that criminalizing nonpayment of child support by making it a misdemeanor or a felony disproportionately affects low-income noncustodial parents who, more likely than not, are just as poor or poorer than the mother and child (or children) owed child support payments.[80] They also contend that criminalizing nonpayment of child support disproportionately affects noncustodial parents who are African American.[81]

Many CSE officials counter that noncustodial parents are not penalized for being poor but rather because they are "deadbeats." They contend that it is about demonstrating intent. They assert that most judges give noncustodial parents chance after chance to avoid jail as long as he or she demonstrates a sincere effort to pay their child support obligation. They maintain that persons who show that they are truly looking for a job—by providing proof that they are filling out applications and talking to prospective employers—and persons who can prove that they have little income by showing documentation of bills and/or income receipts usually succeed in convincing the court that they should not be put in jail, especially if they acknowledge their child support responsibilities and a willingness to meet those obligations.[82]

Some observers argue that although it is not a crime to be poor, if a noncustodial parent is not able to pay his or her child support obligation because he or she has no income, that noncustodial parent could land in jail. They say that although some people assert that jail is the place for deadbeat dads, the truth is that you do not have to be a deadbeat to end up in jail. They claim that if a noncustodial parent is unemployed and unable to meet his or her child support obligation, he or she may be lumped into the deadbeat category.[83] Thus, they contend that many law-abiding citizens face loss of freedom for failing to pay child support because they are poor.[84]

Some noncustodial parents claim that the deck is stacked against them. Many assert that their freedom is in the hands of CSE caseworkers. They contend that when a caseworker feels that enough time has been spent on trying to obtain payment, the caseworker has the authority to have a warrant issued to bring the noncustodial parent before a judge. They note that some noncustodial parents have the misfortune of being arrested and placed in jail immediately following the court proceeding.[85] Many of these noncustodial parents say that it does not seem to them that all other options are used before CSE caseworkers send their cases to the courts for adjudication.

Unlike other felons, noncustodial parents who are put in jail because of nonpayment of child support cannot get credit for child support owed for the time they serve in jail. In other words, a noncustodial parent cannot substitute time in jail in place of making child support payments.[86] Also, as discussed earlier, unlike other felons, most noncustodial parents who face jail time because of noncompliance with child support orders do not get a chance to speak to an attorney or to have an attorney speak on their behalf.[87]

Some observers maintain that incarceration isolates parents from their children and weakens parent-child bonds. They point to the social science literature that maintains that children who have a healthy relationship with both biological parents generally do better on a variety of social indicators than those who only interact with one parent. They note that the costs of incarceration are high and include much more than food, clothing, and shelter expenses. These observers argue that the social, psychological, and emotional impacts on children and families and the negative, disruptive impacts on communities should also be considered. They further maintain that persons with a criminal record have a hard time finding employment and thus a vicious cycle is started and continues.[88] In recent years, the concept of mandating work and/or training programs for low-income noncustodial parents who cannot afford to pay their child support obligations has been viewed by some as an alternative to incarceration.

Other observers say that noncustodial parents are given numerous chances to pay their child support obligation or meet the court's requirements before they are finally remanded to jail or prison. They point out that noncustodial parents who are unable to meet their child support obligation can request a downward modification of their child support order.[89] They contend that in many instances, the CSE agency will negotiate a payment plan with the noncustodial parent and in some instances forgive some of the child support arrearages.[90] They assert that there are many ill-effects that result from failure to pay child support, namely the reduced income/economic status of children. They contend that not meeting child support obligations is a crime and should be treated as such.[91]

Others point out that operating safe, secure, humane, and well-programmed prisons cannot be done inexpensively.[92] They contend that people are incarcerated for legitimate reasons and assert that nonpayment of child support is a legitimate reason for incarceration. They maintain that the cost of incarceration should not be an overriding factor if there is agreement that a crime has been committed.

PLACING THE IMPRISONMENT OPTION IN POLICY CONTEXT

As mentioned earlier, imprisonment of noncustodial parents who are delinquent in making their child support payments is one of the older remedies that state CSE agencies are authorized to use for enforcing child support. Now, especially pursuant to the 1996 welfare reform law (P.L. 104- 193), there are many more child support enforcement tools. Nonetheless, incarceration still remains among the tools used by the CSE program to enforce child support obligations.

Discussions that occurred during the early years of the CSE program indicate that policymakers and administrators maintained that the threat of jail would be more than enough to persuade noncustodial parents to pay their outstanding child support debts—that noncustodial parents would pay rather than go to jail. The historical view was that the CSE program needed "sticks" for noncustodial parents who failed to meet their child support obligations. Many observers viewed imprisonment as the last resort and encouraged CSE administrators to give noncustodial parents several opportunities to comply with child support orders before punishing noncompliant offenders by sending their cases to court, which could result in their incarceration. In practice, this viewpoint is still held. As shown in *Table A-1* in the *Appendix,* all states have criminal sanctions for failure to pay child support.

It used to be that most noncustodial parents who were penalized with jail were there because they were trying to avoid their financial and moral obligations to pay child support for their children.

They tried to hide themselves by moving from place to place or earn money "under the table" (i.e., in the underground economy). Some noncustodial parents have indicated that they did these things out of anger or spite because of animosity toward the children's mother and/or because they believed that the CSE agency was unfairly taking too much out of their meager income.[93]

The CSE program has become more effective and efficient over the years. The program's ability to locate noncustodial parents and their income and assets is well known. Thus, for many noncustodial parents who currently end up in jail because of nonpayment of child support violations, it is because they do not have the income or means to pay. As one analyst put it, they are dead poor, not deadbeats.[94] Other commentators have noted that large CSE caseloads lead to an increased likelihood that noncustodial parents will be viewed as "all the same," as making excuses, and as not trustworthy in their stated reasons for being unable to pay child support.[95] This increases the probability that many low-income noncustodial parents will end up in jail for nonpayment of child support.

Many observers argue that incarcerating people—knowing (1) the high costs associated with imprisoning people and (2) that it may significantly diminish their future ability to get jobs, pay taxes, and lift themselves and their families out of poverty—does not make sense.[96]

Although many custodial parents agree, to a certain extent, that some noncustodial parents are "dead broke" rather than "deadbeats," they contend that the states and the federal government need to proceed with caution in lowering child support orders for low-income noncustodial parents and refusing to use the incarceration option. They argue that child support is a source of income that could mean the difference between poverty and self-sufficiency for some families. They emphasize that lowering the child support order is likely to result in lower income for the child. They argue that even if a noncustodial parent is in dire financial straits, he or she should not be totally released from financial responsibility for the children. They assert that it is imperative that the children not be short-changed, and that children not be made to suffer because of recalcitrant noncustodial parents who fail to meet child support obligations.[97]

According to the National Child Support Enforcement Strategic Plan: "Preventing the build-up of unpaid support (arrearages) through early intervention rather than traditional debt threshold-based enforcement" has been a recent objective and strategy of the CSE program. "That is, we built a system that intervened only after debt ... accumulated and often too late for collection to be successful, let alone of real value to the child. Severe enforcement remedies applied when necessary have their place. But this Strategic Plan signals our intent to build a culture of compliance, in which parents support their children voluntarily and reliably."[98] The CSE Strategic Plan lists the following as ways to strengthen the CSE system and thereby avoid the jail option:

1. modify orders to ensure that obligations stay consistent with ability to pay;[99]
2. contact noncustodial parents soon after a scheduled payment is missed;
3. update child support guidelines to recognize modern family dynamics and realities (e.g., shared custody, incomes of custodial parents, etc.);
4. use automation to detect noncompliance as early as possible; and
5. aim primarily at consistent, reliable payment of current support, even if it means compromising uncollectible arrears to bring the noncustodial parent back into the fold.[100]

Many observers maintain that an effective modification process can help assure that child support orders remain appropriate and prevent the accumulation of inappropriate child support debt.[101] Under the CSE program, states are given significant latitude regarding modifications and reviews of child support orders.[102] Federal law requires that states give both parents the opportunity to request a review of their child support order at least once every three years, and states are required to notify the parents of this right.[103] In order to prevent child support arrearages, especially for noncustodial parents who are unemployed or in prison, some analysts argue that child support modification laws should be changed so that they are more sensitive to periods of incarceration, unemployment, or injury/illness during which the noncustodial parent's ability to pay child support decreases. They contend that it is virtually impossible for most low-income noncustodial parents with those types of barriers to stay current in meeting their monthly child support payments.[104]

In addition, it has periodically been suggested that in some cases in which the child support obligation cannot be met, in-kind assistance (such as providing child care) may be one way in which society can steadfastly adhere to the tenet that both parents are responsible for the well-being of their children while recognizing the reality of the dire financial situation in which many low-income noncustodial parents find themselves.[105]

A wide body of research indicates that father absence has negative ramifications for children.[106] Given that incarceration separates parents from children, many analysts contend that severe enforcement remedies such as incarceration no longer serve a useful purpose. They assert that more innovative approaches to confinement such as probation, participation in drug abuse prevention programs, participation in work and training programs, house arrest, or placement in a halfway house are effective counter measures to the negative effects incarceration has on familial relationships and one's ability to obtain employment.

According to one former inmate: "When you come out of prison, you are facing a lot of issues like housing and transportation. Plus, you're a felon, and it's hard to find work. And you've got to pay child support and the court fees you owe."[107] Many observers contend that non-incarceration remedies are a better option for noncustodial parents, children, families, and ultimately the communities in which they live.[108]

The costs of using the criminal justice system for nonviolent offenders are high. The money from revamping/restructuring the criminal justice system might fund many alternatives. According to the Pew Center on the States, "With states facing the worst fiscal crisis in a generation and corrections costs consuming one in every 15 state discretionary dollars, the need to find cost-effective ways to protect public safety is more critical than ever."[109] Research from the Public Safety Performance Project and its partners details strategies—such as strengthening community supervision and reinvesting money currently spent on imprisoning the lowest risk inmates—to cut corrections costs and give taxpayers a better return on public safety dollars.[110]

There are now many state and federal initiatives with the purpose of trying to ameliorate some of the harmful impacts of father absence. Such initiatives include responsible fatherhood programs and CSE access and visitation programs. These initiatives are intended to provide low-income noncustodial parents with jobs, job training, and/or job skills so that they can earn a living and be able to meet their child support obligations—based on the premise that these noncustodial parents need extra help because people with a prison record are less desirable workers than people who have not been in jail from the standpoint of employers.

Policymakers, CSE analysts and administrators, and most commentators agree that imposing jail time on low-income noncustodial parents who cannot afford to meet their child support obligations can be counterproductive, since imposing jail time means the person is not working and earning money. Moreover, having a criminal record usually lowers a person's job prospects.

Ex-offenders re-entering communities face a host of problems, a major one being barriers to employment because of their criminal records.[111] Most employers now conduct background checks, with the result that people are often denied employment or even fired from jobs because of their criminal records.

Moreover, the inability of many people released from jails and prisons to meet their financial obligations can contribute to their being incarcerated again.[112]

According to a 2005 report:

> For most of these parents, their support orders will not be reduced while they are incarcerated and (unless they find some other means of continuing to pay during their incarceration), they will accumulate arrears and interest on these arrears. Moreover, in most states, if the custodial parent and child receive public assistance, the child support arrears are not owed to the child and custodial parents but to the state, and thus are of no direct benefit to the child, and cannot be forgiven by the custodial parent.
>
> The long-term consequences of these practices on individuals can be enormous. Whether they have been incarcerated for nonpayment of child support or on other grounds, the fact of having been incarcerated and having a criminal record, coupled with a large debt that can quickly reach an unpayable amount can make it virtually impossible for noncustodial parents to secure and maintain employment or to establish stability upon release. The lack of employment and continuing escalation of debt in turn greatly increase the likelihood that the noncustodial parents will be re-incarcerated for nonpayment of child support.[113]

Some commentators maintain that if required work and/or job training programs are used instead of the jail option, noncustodial parents and their children are better off. One CSE enforcement tool that can be used for noncustodial parents who have a child who receives Temporary Assistance for Needy Families (TANF) benefits allows judges to remand nonpaying noncustodial parents (of a child receiving TANF benefits) to a TANF work program, with the mandate to participate in the program, pay the child support owed, or be confined in jail.[114]

This obligation can be monitored to ensure compliance by the noncustodial parent. If the parent is in fact working surreptitiously, it is likely that the work program will conflict with his or her other job, forcing the parent to admit to having earnings and thereby to pay child support. If the noncustodial parent really is jobless, the program can help him or her get a job.

One example of a child support-driven employment project is the Texas Noncustodial Parent Choices Program.[115] Another example is the Fathering Court, which was first implemented in Missouri in 1998 and later launched in Alabama, Iowa, Louisiana, Texas, and Washington, DC. It is an alternative to the prosecution and incarceration of noncustodial fathers with significant child support arrearages.[116]

In addition, some noncustodial parents are participating in Transitional Jobs programs. Transitional Jobs programs provide time-limited wage-paying jobs that combine work, skill development, and supportive services to help participants, who have struggled to find or keep a job, quickly and successfully enter the labor force.[117]

Moreover, a number of state CSE programs have established employment programs in partnership with state and local workforce development boards and local courts for low-income noncustodial parents trying to meet their child support obligations.[118] According to data from the federal Office of Child Support Enforcement (OCSE), as of September 2011, at least 29 states and the District of Columbia were operating work-oriented programs for noncustodial parents with active CSE agency involvement. Most of the programs were not statewide.[119]

However, other observers pose the "what if" question. They wonder what would happen if mandatory work and training program were imposed on low-income noncustodial parents who are unable to pay their child support obligations and for whatever reason these parents are not contributing to their child's support after participating in such a program. Would not incarceration be an appropriate option for low-income noncustodial parents who flunked out of an imposed work/training program, dropped out of the program, or could not keep the provided job?

They contend that incarceration as a penalty of last resort for nonpayment of child support is a logical and long-standing option given that noncustodial parents (like custodial parents) have a moral and financial obligation to support their children and not meeting that obligation is criminal and may have long-term negative consequences for their children. They note the fact that all 50 states and the District of Columbia have criminal sanctions for nonpayment of child support is not happenstance.

APPENDIX. STATE LAWS

The failure to pay child support has been a crime in most states for many years. In the beginning, most of the laws were on the books but in practice rarely used. In the 1990s, nonpayment of child support was viewed as a serious crime. Many states even had a "most wanted" list for child support debtors. Moreover, a 1992 law also made nonpayment of child support a federal crime. By the late 1990s, most states had begun using jail as a last resort option after other CSE enforcement tools proved ineffective.

Table A-1 shows state statutes related to criminal sanctions for failure to pay child support. As seen in the table, the classifications of these statutes include such titles as nonsupport, abandonment of dependent child, desertion and nonsupport of children, flagrant nonsupport, and criminal nonsupport. The maximum penalty ranges from up to six months in jail in Rhode Island and the District of Columbia to a fine of up to $150,000 in Arizona and imprisonment between five and 20 years in Arkansas.

Table A-1 is an update of a table published in 1993 by the HHS Office of Child Support Enforcement in a now defunct publication titled the *Child Support Prosecutor's Bulletin*, which was published quarterly in coordination with the American Bar Association's Child Support Project. This update was compiled by Meredith Peterson and Carla Berry of the Knowledge Services Group of the Congressional Research Service (CRS).

Table A-1. State Criminal Sanctions for Failure to Pay Child Support

State	Citation	Classification	Maximum Penalty
Alabama	Code of Ala. §13A- 13-4	Nonsupport	Class A misdemeanor; fine of up to $6,000, imprisonment for up to one year.
Alaska	Alaska Stat. §11.51.120	Nonsupport	Class C felony; fine of up to $50,000, imprisonment for up to five years.
Arizona	A.R.S. §25-511	Failure of parent to provide for child	Class 6 felony; fine of up to $150,000, imprisonment for up to two years.
Arkansas	A.C.A. §5-26-401	Nonsupport	Class B felony; fine of up to $15,000, imprisonment between five and 20 years.
California	Cal. Pen. Code §270	Failure to provide for child	Misdemeanor; fine of up to $2,000, imprisonment for up to one year, or both.

State	Citation	Classification	Maximum Penalty
Colorado	C.R.S. 14-6-101	Nonsupport	Class 5 felony; fine of between $1,000 and $100,000, imprisonment for up to two years, or both.
Connecticut	Conn. Gen. Stat. §53-304	Nonsupport	Imprisonment for up to one year.
Delaware	11 Del. C. §1113	Aggravated criminal nonsupport	Class G felony; imprisonment for up to two years.
District of Columbia	D.C. Code §46-225.02	Criminal contempt remedy for failure to pay child support	Up to 180 days in jail.
Florida	Fla. Stat. §827.06	Nonsupport	Third degree felony; fine of up to $5,000, imprisonment for up to five years, or both.
Georgia	O.C.G.A. §19-10-1	Abandonment of dependent child	Felony; imprisonment between one and three years.
Hawaii	HRS §709-903	Persistent nonsupport	Misdemeanor; imprisonment for up to one year.
Idaho	Idaho Code §18-401	Desertion and nonsupport of children	Felony; fine of up to $500, imprisonment for up to 14 years, or both.
Illinois	750 ILCS §16/15	Failure to support	Class 4 felony; fine of up to $25,000, imprisonment for one year, or both.
Indiana	Burns Ind. Code Ann. §35-46-1-5	Nonsupport of a child	Class C felony; imprisonment for two to eight years, may be fined up to $10,000.
Iowa	Iowa Code §726.5	Nonsupport	Class D felony; imprisonment for up to five years and fine between $750 and $7,500.
Kansas	K.S.A. §21-3605 (new codification: 21-5606(a)(1))	Nonsupport of a child	Level 10 nonperson felony; presumptive sentence is probation for five to seven years according to the Kansas nondrug sentencing grid.
Kentucky	KRS §530.050	Flagrant nonsupport	Class D felony; fine of between $1,000 and $10,000, imprisonment for one to five years.
Louisiana	La. R.S. 14:74	Criminal neglect of family	Imprisonment for up to six months, fine of $500, or both.
Maine	17-A M.R.S. §552	Nonsupport of dependents	Class E crime; imprisonment for up to six months, fine of up to $1,000.
Maryland	Md. Family Law Code Ann. §10-203	Nonsupport of and desertion of minor child	Misdemeanor; fine of up to $100, imprisonment for up to three years, or both.

Table A-1. (Continued)

State	Citation	Classification	Maximum Penalty
Massachusetts	ALM GL ch. 273, §1	Nonsupport	Felony; carries a fine of up to $10,000, imprisonment in state prison for up to 10 years, or both.
Michigan	MCL §750.161	Neglect to provide shelter, food, care, and clothing	Felony; imprisonment for one to three years in a state correctional facility or county jail for three months to one year.
Minnesota	Minn. Stat. §609.375	Nonsupport	Felony; fine of up to $5,000, imprisonment for up to two years, or both.
Mississippi	Miss. Code Ann. §97-5-3	Nonsupport	Felony; fine between $100 and $500, imprisonment for up to five years, or both.
Missouri	§568.040 R.S. Mo.	Criminal nonsupport	Class D felony; imprisonment for up to four years, fine of up to $5,000.
Montana	Mont. Code Anno. §45-5-621	Aggravated nonsupport	Imprisonment for up to 10 years, fine of up to $50,000, or both.
Nebraska	R.R.S. Neb. §28-706	Criminal nonsupport	Class IV felony; imprisonment up to five years, $10,000 fine, or both.
Nevada	Nev. Rev. Stat. Ann. §201.020	Nonsupport	Category C felony; imprisonment between one and five years, court may also impose fine of up to $10,000.
New Hampshire	RSA 639:4	Nonsupport	Class B felony; imprisonment for up to seven years, fine of up to $4,000, or both.
New Jersey	N.J. Stat. §2C:24-5	Willful nonsupport	Crime in the 4th degree; fine of up to $10,000, imprisonment for up to 18 months.
New Mexico	N.M. Stat. Ann. §30-6-2	Abandonment of dependent	Fourth degree felony; imprisonment for 18 months, court may also impose a fine of u to $5,000.
New York	NY CLS Penal §260.05	Nonsupport of a child in the second degree	Class A misdemeanor; imprisonment for up to one year, fine of up to $1,000.
North Carolina	N.C. Gen. Stat. § 14-322 and § 49-2	Abandonment and failure to support spouse and children	Class 2 misdemeanor; imprisonment for up to 30 days, fine of up to $1,000, or both.
North Dakota	N.D. Cent. Code, 14-07-15	Abandonment or nonsupport of child	Class C felony; fine of $5,000; imprisonment for up to five years, or both.

State	Citation	Classification	Maximum Penalty
Ohio	ORC Ann. 2919.21	Nonsupport or contributing to nonsupport of dependents	Felony of the 5th degree; imprisonment between six and 12months, fine of up to $2,500.
Oklahoma	21 Ok. St. §851	Desertion of children under age of 10 a felony; Omission to provide for a child	Desertion is a felony punishable by imprisonment for one to 10 years. Omission to provide is a felony punishable by imprisonment for up to four years, a fine up to $5,000, or both.
Oregon	ORS §163.555	Criminal nonsupport	Class C felony; fine of up to $125,000, imprisonment for up to five years.
Pennsylvania	23 Pa. C.S. §4354	Willful failure to pay support order	Misdemeanor of the 3rd degree; imprisonment for up to one year, fine of up to $2,500,
Rhode Island	R.I. Gen. Laws §11-2-1	Abandonment or nonsupport of spouse or children	Misdemeanor; imprisonment for up to six months.
South Carolina	S.C. Children's Code §63-5-20	Obligation to support	Misdemeanor; imprisonment for up to one year, fine of between $300 and $1,500, or both.
South Dakota	S.D. Codified Laws §25-7-16, 17	Failure to support child	Class 6 felony; fine of up to $4,000, imprisonment for up to two years, or both.
Tennessee	Tenn. Code Ann. §39-15-101	Flagrant nonsupport	Class E felony; imprisonment between one and six years, jury also may assess a fine of up to $3,000.
Texas	Tex. Penal Code §25.05	Criminal nonsupport	State jail felony; imprisonment between 180 days and two years and a fine of up to $10,000.
Utah	Utah Code Ann. §76-7-201	Criminal nonsupport	Felony of the 3rd degree; imprisonment for up to five years, fine of up to $5,000.
Vermont	15 V.S.A. §202	Penalty for desertion or nonsupport	Imprisonment for up to two years, fine of up to $300, or both.
Virginia	Va. Code Ann. §20-61	Desertion or nonsupport of wife, husband, or children	Misdemeanor; fine of up to $500, imprisonment for up to one year, or both.

Table A-1. (Continued)

State	Citation	Classification	Maximum Penalty
Washington	Rev. Code Wash. (ARCW) §26.20.030and §26.20.035	Family abandonment and nonsupport	Abandonment is a Class C felony; fine up to $10,000, imprisonment for up to five years, or both. Nonsupport is a gross misdemeanor; fine of up to $5,000, imprisonment for up to 364 days, or both.
West Virginia	W. Va. Code §61-5-29	Failure to meet an obligation to provide support to a minor	Felony; fine between $100 to $1,000, imprisonment between one and three years, or both.
Wisconsin	Wis. Stat. §948.22	Failure to support	Class I felony; fine of up to $10,000, imprisonment for up to three years and six months, or both.
Wyoming	Wyo. Stat. §20-3-101	Desertion of spouse or children	Misdemeanor; fine of up to $1,000, imprisonment between seven days and one year, or both.

Source: Table compiled by the Congressional Research Service, based on a table published in 1993 by the Office of Child Support Enforcement in conjunction with the American Bar Association.

Notes: Maximum penalties shown are for first-time offenders. In states that classify nonsupport as a more serious offense due to factors such as amount of arrearage, length of time arrearage is owed, or existence of a court order for support, the most serious offense and the maximum sentence are listed.

End Notes

[1] For general information on the CSE program, see CRS Report RS22380, Child Support Enforcement: Program Basics, by Carmen Solomon-Fears.

[2] Note: This report primarily uses the term incarceration without mentioning whether the confinement is in a jail or a prison. Jails are correctional facilities that confine persons before or after adjudication of a case or confine individuals who have been convicted of a misdemeanor offense. Jails generally are operated by local law enforcement authorities. Jail sentences are usually for one year or less. Noncustodial parents who are incarcerated for violations related to nonpayment of child support are usually put in jail rather than prison. Although this is usually the case, it is not always handled this way. In some states, nonpayment of child support is a felony and noncustodial parents convicted of felony nonsupport charges usually are sent to prison. Prisons are operated by the state government or by the federal government. Persons serving a sentence of more than a year are usually put in prison.

[3] The Urban Institute, Assessing Child Support Arrears in Nine Large States and the Nation, by Elaine Sorensen, Liliana Sousa, and Simon Schaner, July 11, 2007.

[4] According to one source, about 50,000 persons are incarcerated daily in U.S. jails and prisons as a result of child support debts. (Source: Douglas Galbi, Persons in Jail or in Prison for Child-Support Debt, March 22, 2011, http://purplemotes.net/2011/03/22/persons-in-jail-for-child-support-debt/.)

[5] For more information, CRS Report R41762, Child Support Enforcement and Driver's License Suspension Policies, by Carmen Solomon-Fears.

[6] In effect, the 1994 Full Faith and Credit for Child Support Orders Act (P.L. 103-383) requires all states and tribes to recognize and enforce a valid child support order of other states and tribes.

[7] 18 U.S.C. §228.

[8] Office of Child Support Enforcement, Child Support Enforcement FY 2010 Preliminary Report, May 2011.

[9] CRS Report R41762, Child Support Enforcement and Driver's License Suspension Policies, by Carmen Solomon-Fears.

[10] William J. Brockelbank, Interstate Enforcement of Family Support (The Runaway Pappy Act), Second Edition by Felix Infausto, 1971, p. 3.

[11] State Laws for Child Support, http://www.child-support-guide.com/state-laws-for-child-support.html.

[12] William J. Brockelbank, Interstate Enforcement of Family Support (The Runaway Pappy Act), Second Edition by Felix Infausto, 1971, p. 17.

[13] During the 106th Congress, Representative Nancy Johnson, then chair of the House Ways and Means Subcommittee on Human Resources, stated, "To take the next step in welfare reform we must find a way to help children by providing them with more than a working mother and sporadic child support." She noted that many low-income fathers have problems similar to those of mothers on welfare—namely, they are likely to have dropped out of high school, to have little work experience, and to have significant barriers that lessen their ability to find and/or keep a job. She also asserted that in many cases these men are "dead broke" rather than "dead beats," and that the federal government should help these noncustodial fathers meet both their financial and emotional obligations to their children. (Source: U.S. Congress, House Ways and Means Subcommittee on Human Resources, "Hearing on Fatherhood Legislation," Statement of Chairman Nancy Johnson, 106th Congress, 1st Session, October 5, 1999, p. 4.)

[14] National Conference of State Legislatures, Case in Brief: Courts Uphold Criminal Penalties for the Failure to Pay Child Support, by Teresa A. Myers.

[15] Enforcement on Non-payment of Child Maintenance in England and Wales, http://www.nidirect.gov.uk/ enforcement-of-non-payment-of-child-maintenance-in-england-and-wales.

[16] Christine Skinner and Jacqueline Davidson, Recent Trends in Child Maintenance Schemes in 14 Countries, International Journal of Law, Policy, and the Family 23, 2009, pp. 25-52, http://lawfam.oxfordjournals.org/content/23/ 1/25.full.pdf+html.

[17] Ibid.

[18] National Conference of State Legislatures, Case in Brief: Courts Uphold Criminal Penalties for the Failure to Pay Child Support, by Teresa A. Myers.

[19] Rebecca May, The Effect of Child Support and Criminal Justice Systems on Low-Income Noncustodial Parents-When You Need a Safety Net, but There's Only a Dragnet, June 2004, p. 9/22.

[20] Rebecca May and Marguerite Roulet, A Look at Arrests of Low-Income Fathers for Child Support Nonpayment: Enforcement, Court and Program Practices, Center for Family Policy

and Practice, January 2005, http://www.cprmn.org/Documents/noncompliance.pdf. See pp. 13-38 for some state-by-state examples.

[21] U.S. Department of Health and Human Services, Office of Child Support Enforcement, Essentials for Attorneys in Child Support Enforcement, 3rd Edition, 2002, Chapter 10, http://www.acf.hhs.gov/programs/cse/pubs/2002/reports/ essentials/. (Hereinafter, "HHS Child Support Essentials.")

[22] International Union, United Mine Workers v. Bagwell, 512 U.S. 821, 827-28 (1994); F.T.C. v. Trudeau, 579 F.3d 754, 769 (7th Cir. 2009)(internal citations omitted)("Generally, civil contempt is remedial and for the benefit of the complainant, while criminal contempt is punitive, to vindicate the authority of the court. In terms of monetary sanctions, civil sanctions fall in two categories. They can compensate the complainant for those losses caused by the contemptuous conduct. Or they can coerce the contemnor's compliance with a court order. A coercive sanction must afford the contemnor the opportunity to purge, meaning the contemnor can avoid punishment by complying with the court order") (internal citations omitted). See also Earl C. Dudley, Jr., Getting Beyond the Civil/Criminal Distinction: A New Approach to the Regulation of Indirect Contempts, 79 Va. L. Rev. 1025, 1038-39 (1993).

[23] United States v. Rangolan, 464 F.3d 321, 325 (2d Cir. 2006).

[24] HHS Child Support Essentials.

[25] Ibid.

[26] In re Bradley, 588 F.3d 254, 263 (5th Cir. 2009)("Imprisonment is an appropriate remedy for either civil or criminal contempt, depending on how it is assessed, if the prison term is conditional and coercive, the character of the contempt is civil; if it is backward-looking and unconditional it is criminal.... Similarly, a fine that punishes past conduct is criminal, while a fine that accrues on an ongoing basis in response to noncompliance is civil"). See also Earl C. Dudley, Jr., Getting Beyond the Civil/Criminal Distinction: A New Approach to the Regulation of Indirect Contempts, 79 Va. L. Rev. 1025, pp. 1038-39 (1993).

[27] HHS Child Support Essentials.

[28] Earl C. Dudley, Jr., Getting Beyond the Civil/Criminal Distinction: A New Approach to the Regulation of Indirect Contempts, 79 Va. L. Rev. 1025, pp. 1038-39 (1993).

[29] Turner v. Rogers, 131 S.Ct. 2507, 2518 (2011), p. 16/33, available at http://www. Supreme ecourt.gov/opinions/10pdf/ 10-10.pdf.

[30] HHS Child Support Essentials.

[31] Ibid.

[32] Ibid.

[33] Ibid.

[34] Ibid.

[35] Ibid.

[36] Hicks v. Feiock, 485 U.S. 624, 638, n.9 (1988). See also: Turner v. Rogers et al., p. 12/33, at http://www.supremecourt.gov/opinions/10pdf/10-10.pdf.

[37] Turner v. Rogers, 131 S.Ct. 2507, 2516 (2011)

[38] Hicks v. Feiock, 485 U.S. at 637-641.

[39] Turner v. Rogers, 131 S.Ct. 2507, 2516 (2011), p. 12/33 (quoting Hicks v. Feiock, 485 U.S. 624 (1988)), http://www.supremecourt.gov/opinions/10pdf/10-10.pdf.

[40] See United States v. Dixon, 509 U.S. 688, 696 (1993)(holding that the Sixth Amendment grants an indigent defendant the right to counsel in criminal cases, including most criminal contempt proceedings).

[41] HHS Child Support Essentials.

[42] Ibid.
[43] Ibid.
[44] 131 S. Ct. 2507 (2011).
[45] Turner at 2519.
[46] http://www.americanbar.org/content/dam/aba/publishing/previewbriefs/ Other_Brief_ Updates /10- 10_Respondent.authcheckdam.pdf.
[47] 424 U.S. 319 (1976).
[48] Turner at 2519.
[49] Turner at 2520.
[50] Turner at 2520.
[51] Ronald B. Mincy and Elaine J. Sorensen, "Deadbeats and Turnips in Child Support Reform," December 7, 1998, Journal of Policy Analysis and Management, vol. 17, issue 1, Winter 1998, pp. 44–51.
[52] In the CSE literature, "deadbeats" is a term sometimes used for noncustodial parents who can afford to pay child support but choose not to do so unless forced. In contrast, "turnips" is a term used to describe noncustodial parents who cannot pay child support because they are too poor. It refers to the saying that "you can't get blood from a turnip." In other words, if they do not have it, you cannot get it.
[53] Ronald B. Mincy and Elaine J. Sorensen, "Deadbeats and Turnips in Child Support Reform," December 7, 1998, Journal of Policy Analysis and Management, vol. 17, issue 1, Winter 1998, pp. 44–51.
[54] Turner v. Rogers et al., Supreme Court, June 20, 2011, p. 18/33, http://www.suprem ecourt.gov/opinions/10pdf/10- 10.pdf.
[55] Ibid, pp.18-20/33.
[56] Price v. Turner, 691 S.E.2d 470 (S.C. 2010)
[57] Turner v. Rogers, p. 20/33. See also Court Ruling Spurs Changes in Child Support Cases, by Rick Brundrett, July 7, 2011.
[58] HHS Child Support Essentials.
[59] Ibid.
[60] U.S. Congress, 102nd Congress, 2nd Session, House of Representatives, Child Support Recovery Act of 1992, Report to Accompany H.R. 1241, August 2, 1992, H. Rept. 102-771, p. 6.
[61] 18 U.S.C. §228(a)(1).
[62] U.S. Department of Health and Human Services, Office of Child Support Enforcement, Child Support Report, vol. XVI, no. 7, "U.S. Attorney's Office Prosecutes Criminal Nonsupport Case," by T.J. Centrella, November 1994.
[63] Congressional Record, Senate, Remarks on S. 1371 by Senator Kohl, November 13, 1997, p. S12667
[64] 18 U.S.C. §228(a)(2) and (3).
[65] Department of Health and Human Services, Office of Child Support Enforcement, Office of Child Support Enforcement FY 2006 Annual Report to Congress, 2007.
[66] Data on the number of persons arrested and sentenced under Project Save Our Children were not made available for FY2007 and no subsequent data on Project Save Our Children are in subsequent annual CSE reports.
[67] Bill Rankin, "'Deadbeat' parents caught in a debtor's prison," Atlanta Journal-Constitution, January 24, 2011.

[68] National Women's Law Center and the Center on Fathers, Families, and Public Policy, Family Ties: Improving Paternity Establishment Practices and Procedures for Low-Income Mothers, Fathers and Children, 2000, pp. 9-11.

[69] Craig Haney, The Psychological Impact of Incarceration: Implications for Post-Prison Adjustment, December 2001, pp. 5-8/16.

[70] Although this is usually the case, it is not always the case. In some states, nonpayment of child support is a felony and noncustodial parents convicted of felony nonsupport charges usually are sent to prison.

[71] Nancy Wolff, Cynthia L. Blitz, Jing Shi, Jane Siegel, and Ronet Bachman, "Physical Violence Inside Prisons: Rates of Victimization," Criminal Justice and Behavior, vol. 34, no. 5, Sage Publications, May 2007, pp. 588-599. See also Mark S. Fleisher and Jessie L. Krienert, The Culture of Prison Sexual Violence, November 2006.

[72] Nancy Wolff, Cynthia L. Blitz, Jing Shi, Jane Siegel, and Ronet Bachman, "Physical Violence Inside Prisons: Rates of Victimization," Criminal Justice and Behavior, vol. 34, no. 5, Sage Publications, May 2007, p. 595.

[73] Dahlia Lithwick, "Our Real Prison Problem—Why are we so worried about Gitmo?", The Daily Beast, June 4, 2009, http://www.thedailybeast.com/newsweek/2009/06/04/our-real-prison-problem.print.html.

[74] American Civil Liberties Union, In For A Penny: The Rise of America's New Debtors' Prisons, October 2010, p. 6, http://www.acluohio.org/issues/ criminaljustice/I nForA Penny.pdf.

[75] Craig Haney, The Psychological Impact of Incarceration: Implications for Post-Prison Adjustment, December 2001.

[76] The Urban Institute, The Impact of Incarceration and Reentry on Children, Families, and Communities, edited by Jeremy Travis and Michelle Waul, 2003. See also Council on Crime and Justice, The Collateral Effects of Incarceration on Fathers, Families, and Communities, March 2006.

[77] Maria Cancian, Daniel R. Meyer, and Eunhee Han, "Child Support: Responsible Fatherhood and the Quid Pro Quo," The Annals of the American Academy of Political and Social Science, vol. 635 no. 1 (140-162), May 2011, p. 151. See also Adam Liptak, "U.S. Imprisons One in 100 Adults, Report Finds," The New York Times.com, February 29, 2008. See also Christian Henrichson and Ruth Delaney, The Price of Prisons-What Incarceration Costs Taxpayers, VERA Institute of Justice, Center on Sentencing and Corrections, January 2012 (updated).

[78] MDRC, Building Knowledge About Successful Prisoner Reentry Strategies, Issue Focus, February 11, 2009.

[79] Justice Policy Institute, Baltimore Behind Bars: How to Reduce the Jail Population, Save Money and Improve Public Safety, June 8, 2010.

[80] Rebecca May and Marguerite Roulet, A Look at Arrests of Low-Income Fathers for Child Support Nonpayment: Enforcement, Court and Program Practices, Center for Family Policy and Practice, January 2005, p. 6, http://www.cprmn.org/Documents/noncompliance.pdf.

[81] Rebecca May, The Effect of Child Support and Criminal Justice Systems on Low-Income Noncustodial Parents— When You Need a Safety Net, but There's Only a Dragnet, June 2004, p. 9. See also Justice Policy Institute, Baltimore Behind Bars: How to Reduce the Jail Population, Save Money and Improve Public Safety, June 8, 2010.

[82] Rebecca May and Marguerite Roulet, A Look at Arrests of Low-Income Fathers for Child Support Nonpayment: Enforcement, Court and Program Practices, Center for Family Policy and Practice, January 2005, p. 6, http://www.cprmn.org/Documents/noncompliance.pdf.

[83] Ibid.

[84] Ibid.

[85] Elizabeth G. Patterson, "Civil Contempt And The Indigent Child Support Obligor: The Silent Return Of Debtor's Prison," Cornell Journal Of Law And Public Policy, vol. 18:95-141, 2008.

[86] Moreover, while the noncustodial parent is incarcerated the child support debt continues to accumulate unless he or she has requested and been granted a modification of the child support order by the CSE agency.

[87] As indicated earlier in the report, noncustodial parents charged with criminal contempt of court are to a certain extent better off than those charged with civil contempt of court because they are entitled to an attorney and other due-process protections.

[88] Sharon M. Dietrich, "Every Door Closed-Barriers Facing Parents With Criminal Records," Criminal Records and Employment: Ex-Offenders Thwarted in Attempts to Earn a Living for Their Families, Center for Law and Social Policy and Community Legal Services, Inc., 2003.

[89] National Conference of State Legislatures, Case in Brief: Courts Uphold Criminal Penalties for the Failure to Pay Child Support, by Teresa A. Myers, June 1999.

[90] Paula Roberts, An Ounce Of Prevention And A Pound Of Cure: Developing State Policy On The Payment of Child Support Arrears by Low Income Parents, Center for Law and Social Policy, May 2001. Note: According to the federal Office of Child Support Enforcement (OCSE), as of September 2011, 44 states and the District of Columbia had policies to compromise child support debt owed to the state, see http://www.acf.hhs.gov/programs/cse/debt_compromise.html.

[91] Department of Health and Human Services, Office of the Inspector General, "Operation Lost and Found nets Chronic Child Support Defaulters," OIG News, September 15, 2003.

[92] Christian Henrichson and Ruth Delaney, The Price of Prisons-What Incarceration Costs Taxpayers, VERA Institute of Justice, Center on Sentencing and Corrections, January 2012 (updated), p. 12.

[93] Maureen Waller and Robert Plotnick, "A Failed Relationship? Low-Income Families And The Child Support Enforcement System," University of Wisconsin–Madison Institute for Research on Poverty, Focus, vol. 21, no. 1, Spring 2000, pp. 12-17.

[94] Elaine Sorensen and Chava Zibman, Poor Dads Who Don't Pay Child Support: Deadbeats or Disadvantaged, Urban Institute, April 2001.

[95] Rebecca May and Marguerite Roulet, A Look at Arrests of Low-Income Fathers for Child Support Nonpayment: Enforcement, Court and Program Practices, Center for Family Policy and Practice, January 2005, p. 46, http://www.cpr-mn.org/Documents/noncompliance.pdf.

[96] Mike Davis, "Illinois prison overcrowding is dangerous for everyone," October 13, 2011, http://www.occasionalplanet.org/2011/10/13/illinois-prison-overcrowding-is-dangerous-for-everyone/print/.

[97] Jennifer L. Noyes, Review of Child Support Policies for Incarcerated Payers, Institute for Research on Poverty, University of Wisconsin-Madison, December 2006. See also Maria Cancian, Daniel R. Meyer, and Eunhee Han, "Child Support: Responsible Fatherhood and the Quid Pro Quo," The Annals of the American Academy of Political and Social Science, vol. 635 no. 1 (140-162), May 2011.

[98] Department of Health and Human Services, National Child Support Enforcement Strategic Plan for FY2005-FY2009, p. 2.

[99] According to the federal Office of Child Support Enforcement (OCSE), as of September 2011, at least 22 states and the District of Columbia were supporting various types of programs

designed to ensure that child support orders reflect current earnings when the order is established and is modified when earnings change. See http://www.acf.hhs.gov/programs/cse/right_sizing_orders.html.

[100] Ibid.

[101] For information on noncustodial parents with high child support arrearages, see Elaine Sorensen, Liliana Sousa, and Simon Schaner, Assessing Child Support Arrears in Nine Large States and the Nation, Urban Institute, July 11, 2007, pp. 19-24, http://aspe.hhs.gov/hsp/07/assessing-CS-debt/.

[102] This flexibility and discretion only applies to prospective modification of child support orders. Federal law prohibits the retroactive modification of child support orders (Section 466(a)(9) of the Social Security Act).

[103] Some observers contend that the CSE program should aggressively advertise its modification process because many noncustodial parents are under the mistaken belief that if they fall behind in their child support payments at a time when they are legitimately unable to make the payments, the amount they owe can later be reduced or discounted by the court when an explanation for nonpayment is given.

[104] Mindy Herman-Stahl, Marni L. Kan, and Tasseli McKay, Incarceration and the Family: A Review of Research and Promising Approaches for Serving Fathers and Families, RTI International, September 2008, pp. 6-4 through-6-6.

[105] Tribal CSE programs, unlike state CSE programs, have the authority to allow noncustodial parents to use in-kind payments instead of cash to satisfy child support debt. For information on Tribal CSE programs, see CRS Report R41204, Child Support Enforcement: Tribal Programs, by Carmen Solomon-Fears.

[106] Wendy Sigle-Rushton and Sara McLanahan, Father Absence and Child Well-Being: A Critical Review, Princeton University, Center for Research on Child Wellbeing (Working Paper #02-20), November 2002.

[107] Ginnie Graham, "Program helps felons meet child support obligations," Tulsa World, December 12, 2011, http://www.tulsaworld.com/news/article.aspx? subjectid=11 & articleid=20111212_11_A1_ULNSea29809.

[108] For more information, see CRS Report R40499, Child Support Enforcement and Ex-Offenders, by Carmen Solomon-Fears.

[109] The Pew Center on the States, One in 100: Behind Bars in America 2008. See also http://www.pewcenteronthestates.org/initiatives_detail.aspx?initiativeID=59068

[110] The Pew Center on the States, Risk/Needs Assessment 101: Science Reveals New Tools to Manage Offenders, September 2011.

[111] Sharon M. Dietrich, "Every Door Closed—Barriers Facing Parents With Criminal Records," Criminal Records and Employment: Ex-Offenders Thwarted in Attempts to Earn a Living for Their Families, Center for Law and Social Policy and Community Legal Services, Inc., 2003.

[112] Katherine A. Beckett, Alexes M. Harris, Heather Evans, The Assessment and Consequences of Legal Financial Obligations in Washington State, Washington State Minority and Justice Commission, August 2008. See also Rebekah Diller, The Hidden Costs of Florida's Criminal Justice Fees, Brennan Center for Justice, 2010.

[113] Rebecca May and Marguerite Roulet, A Look at Arrests of Low-Income Fathers for Child Support Nonpayment: Enforcement, Court and Program Practices, Center for Family Policy and Practice, January 2005, p. 46, http://www.cpr-mn.org/Documents/noncompliance.pdf.

[114] 42 U.S.C. §666(a)(15).

[115] The Texas Noncustodial Parents (NCP) Choices Program provides enhanced child support case compliance monitoring and employment services for noncustodial parents linked to a TANF/Medicaid case who are unemployed or underemployed and are not compliant with their child support obligations. Participation in the program is mandatory as ordered by CSE associate judges in the 14 sites currently funded by the Texas Workforce Commission and the Office of Attorney General (OAG). NCP Choices launched three new sites and expanded one existing site in spring 2010. According to the Texas CSE website, noncustodial parents ordered into NCP Choices have, on average, made no payments in the eight months prior to program entry and pay an average of $176 per month in the first year after program entry. Evaluation results show this as an overall 57% increase in child support payments for noncustodial parents participating in this program as compared to a control group of similar noncustodial parents in the OAG caseload, http://www.oag.state.tx.us/cs/ofi/index.shtml.

[116] "Noncustodial fathers who are in arrears with their child support have their criminal prosecution deferred while they participate in Fathering Court. This experience starts with a needs assessment and the development of an action plan by the father and a case manager to help the dad become a more responsible father. Community partners provide priority services to the dad [such as job training and employment] while he participates in fathering classes that use a tested curriculum. Classes equip him with knowledge and skills to become the father his child needs. When the father completes his action plan, the prosecution is dismissed." (Source: National Center for Fathering, Fathering Court-Getting To The Heart Of Child Support, Fathers.com, December 2009, p. 5.)

[117] The Employment and Training Administration (ETA) in the U.S. Department of Labor is currently sponsoring the Enhanced Transitional Jobs Demonstration (ETJD), which is designed to fund and rigorously test employment programs targeting noncustodial parents and individuals recently released from prison. The following seven grantees are participating in the demonstration: (1) Center for Community Alternatives, Syracuse, NY; (2) Goodwill of North Georgia, Atlanta, GA; (3) City and County of San Francisco, CA; (4) Tarrant County Workforce Development Board, Fort Worth, TX; (5) The Doe Fund Inc., New York, NY; (6) Workforce Inc., Indianapolis, IN; and (7) Young Women's Christian Association of Greater Milwaukee, WI. The following organizations are developing and implementing a random assignment framework for the demonstration and will evaluate the programs: MDRC, Abt Associates, and MEF Associates. (Source: MDRC, The Enhanced Transitional Jobs Demonstration, http://www.mdrc.org/ project_25_106.html.)

[118] Department of Health and Human Services, Office of Child Support Enforcement, Noncustodial Parents: Summaries of Research, Grants and Practices, July 2009. See also Shane Spaulding, Jean Baldwin Grossman, and Dee Wallace, Working Dads: Final Report on the Fathers at Work Initiative, Public/Private Ventures, 2009.

[119] Office of Child Support Enforcement, Work-Oriented Programs for Noncustodial Parents with Active Child Support Agency Involvement, 2012, http://www.acf.hhs.gov/programs/cse/work_oriented.html.

In: Child Support Issues
Editor: Rene Pellerin
ISBN: 978-1-62808-376-7

Chapter 3

CHILD SUPPORT: AN OVERVIEW OF CENSUS BUREAU DATA ON RECIPIENTS*

Carmen Solomon-Fears

SUMMARY

The national Census Bureau data show that in 2009, nearly 13.7 million parents had custody of children under age 21 while the other parent lived elsewhere, and the aggregate amount of child support received was $21.4 billion. In 2009, 82% of custodial parents were mothers. Of all custodial parents, 52% were white, 25% were black, 19% were Hispanic, 18% were married, 34% were divorced, 35% were never married, 15% did not have a high school diploma, 17% had at least a bachelor's degree, 50% worked full-time year-round, 28% had family income below poverty, and 38% received some type of public assistance. In 2009, only 2.4 million (35%) of the 6.9 million custodial parents with child support orders actually received the full amount of child support that was owed to them. The average yearly child support payment received by custodial parents with payments was $5,248 for mothers and $4,202 for fathers. These full or partial payments represented 17% of the custodial mothers' total yearly income and 10% of the custodial fathers'. Compared to 1993 Census data, less child support was received by custodial parents in 2009 ($22.8 billion in 1993 versus $21.4 billion in

* This is an edited, reformatted and augmented version of a Congressional Research Service publication, CRS Report for Congress RS22499, prepared for Members and Committees of Congress, from www.crs.gov, dated December 16, 2011.

2009; in 2009 dollars). However, a higher percentage of those owed child support actually received all that they were due (36.9% in 1993 versus 41.2% in 2009).

INTRODUCTION

The United States Census Bureau periodically collects national survey information on child support. By interviewing a random sample of single-parent families, the Census Bureau is able to generate an array of data that is useful in assessing the performance of noncustodial parents in paying their child support. Although the Census Bureau has been collecting child support information in a special Child Support Supplement to the April Current Population Survey (CPS) biennially since 1978, the supplement survey has changed significantly over the years. According to the Census Bureau, the most recent data, from 2009,[1] are comparable only back to 1993. During the early years of the survey, information was collected only from custodial mothers. Beginning with the 1991 data, information was also collected from custodial fathers. This report presents unsegmented data with respect to custodial mothers and fathers (i.e., custodial parents data). The survey population includes all persons who have their own children under age 21 living with them, while the other parent lives outside the household.

The Child Support Enforcement (CSE) program was enacted in 1975 as a federal-state program (Title IV-D of the Social Security Act) to help strengthen families by securing financial support for children from their noncustodial parent on a consistent and continuing basis, and by helping some families to remain self-sufficient and off public assistance by providing the requisite CSE services. The CSE program is administered by the Office of Child Support Enforcement (OCSE) in the Department of Health and Human Services (HHS), and funded by general revenues. All 50 states, the District of Columbia, Guam, Puerto Rico, and the Virgin Islands operate CSE programs and are entitled to federal matching funds. The CSE program provides seven major services on behalf of children: (1) parent location, (2) paternity establishment, (3) establishment of child support orders, (4) review and modification of child support orders, (5) collection of child support payments, (6) distribution of child support payments, and (7) establishment and enforcement of medical child support. The CSE program is estimated to handle at least 50% of all child support cases; the remaining cases are handled by private attorneys, collection agencies, or through mutual agreements between the parents.

In FY2009, the CSE program collected $26.4 billion in child support payments (from noncustodial parents) and served 15.8 million child support cases. The national Census Bureau data show that the aggregate amount of child support received in 2009 was $21.4 billion,[2] and that 13.7 million parents had custody of children under age 21 while the other parent lived elsewhere.[3]

In 2009, 82% of custodial parents were mothers. Of all custodial parents, 52% were white, 25% were black, 19% were Hispanic, 18% were married, 34% were divorced, 35% were never married, 15% did not have a high school diploma, 17% had at least a bachelor's degree, 50% worked full-time year-round, 28% had family income below poverty, and 38% received some type of public assistance (i.e., Medicaid, food stamps, public housing or rent subsidy, TANF, or general assistance).

Child Support Awarded and Received

Table 1 summarizes several child support indicators from biennial survey data for selected years from 1993 through 2009. The table shows that the likelihood of having a child support award, being legally entitled to a child support payment, and actually receiving at least one child support payment decreased over the 17-year period from 1993 through 2007. In contrast, the percentage of noncustodial parents (owed child support) who received the full amount of the child support that they were owed increased by about 12%, from 37% in 1993 to 41% in 2009.

In 2009, about 51% of the nearly 13.7 million custodial parents (with children under age 21) were awarded child support.[4] Of those who were actually *due* child support payments (5.9 million), about 71% of them received at least one payment, and 41% received all that they were owed. In 2009, only 2.4 million (18%) of the 13.7 million custodial parents *eligible* for child support actually received the full amount of child support that was owed to them. In 2009, the average child support payment amounted to about $3,629,[5] 10% higher than the average child support payment in 1993 ($3,289).

In 2009, 61% of the $35 billion in aggregate child support due was actually paid. In 1993, 65% of the $35 billion (adjusted for inflation, in 2009 dollars) in child support due was paid. During the 15-year period 1993 through 2009, after adjusting for inflation, aggregate child support due fluctuated from a low of $34.9 billion in 1993 to a high of $43.2 billion in 2003.

Table 1. Child Support Award and Receipt, 1993-2009

	1993	1995	1997	1999	2001	2003	2005	2007	2009	PercentChange (1993-2009)
All custodial parents (numbers in thousands)	13,690	13,715	13,949	13,529	13,383	13,951	13,605	13,743	13,672	-0.1
Custodial parents awarded child support (thousands)	7,800	7,967	7,876	7,945	7,916	8,376	7,802	7,428	6,914	-11.4
Percent awarded child support	57.0	58.1	56.5	58.7	59.1	60.0	57.3	54.0	50.6	-5.3
Custodial parents due/owed child support (numbers in thousands)	6,688	6,958	7,018	6,791	6,924	7,256	6,809	6,375	5,897	-11.8
Percent of those owed who received any payment	75.8	75.7	75.3	73.7	73.9	76.5	77.2	76.3	70.8	-6.6
Percent of those owed who received full payment	36.9	42.3	46.2	45.1	44.7	45.3	46.9	46.8	41.2	11.7
Average child support due	$5,234	$5,684	$5,527	$6,121	$6,111	$5,952	$6,135	$5,534	$5,955	13.8
Average child support received	$3,417	$3,745	$3,683	$3,593	$3,828	$4,081	$4,003	$3,470	$3,634	6.4
		Aggregate Child Support Payments (in billions of dollars)								
Child support due	$34.9	$39.5	$38.8	$41.6	$42.3	$43.2	$41.8	$35.3	$35.1	0.6
Child support received	$22.8	$26.0	$25.9	$24.5	$26.5	$29.6	$27.2	$22.1	$21.4	-6.1
Child support deficit	$12.1	$13.6	$12.9	$17.1	$15.8	$13.5	$14.5	$13.1	$13.7	13.2
Percent of amount due actually received	65.3%	65.7%	66.7%	58.8%	62.8%	68.6%	65.3%	62.8%	61.0%	-6.6

Source: Table prepared by the Congressional Research Service (CRS), based on data from the U.S. Census Bureau, Current Population Survey, April 1994-2010. All child support income amounts were adjusted to reflect 2009 dollars using the CPI-U-RS. Custodial parents include all persons living with their own children who are under age 21 while the other parent lives somewhere else.

Note: The difference between the number of custodial parents who were awarded child support and those who were due or owed child support is composed of persons who were no longer owed child support because their child was (or children were) too old, the noncustodial parent had died, the family lived together for part of the year before the survey interview, or some other reason. (To clarify, in 2009, 6.9 million custodial parents were awarded child support, but only 5.9 million were due (or owed) child support. The 1.0 million-person difference was composed of persons who were no longer due child support because of the reasons listed above.)

But, over the entire period, aggregate child support due increased less than 1%, total child support received decreased by about 6%, and the amount left unpaid increased 13% (see *Table 1*).

Demographic and Economic Characteristics of Custodial Parents Who Were Awarded or Who Received Child Support Payments in 2009

While sex, race, marital status, and education are significant factors in predicting whether a custodial parent will be issued a child support order, award rates tend to be significantly lower than receipt rates. For example, although female custodial parents were 1.8 times as likely to be awarded child support in 2009 as their male counterparts, among parents who were owed/due child support, both had at least a 70% chance of actually receiving child support payments. (See *Table 2.)* Moreover, in 2009, 45% of black custodial parents were awarded child support compared to 56% of white custodial parents. Even so, 62% of black custodial parents who were owed/due child support actually received child support payments and 73% of white custodial parents who were owed child support actually received child support payments in 2009. Similarly, while only 44% of never-married parents were awarded child support in 2009, 66% of never-married parents who were owed child support actually received child support payments in 2009. Also, 42% of custodial parents without a high school diploma were awarded child support, while 59% of custodial parents without a high school diploma who were owed child support actually received child support.

This pattern also held for the economic factors listed in *Table 2*—in that once a child support obligation was awarded, the probability of actually receiving payments rose significantly for all categories of custodial parents. In 2009, 47% of custodial parents with incomes below the poverty level were awarded child support, and 66% of those owed/due payments actually received child support payments. *Table 2* also shows that 52% of custodial parents who worked full-time year-round were awarded child support, while 72% of those owed received child support payments. Similarly, about 49% of custodial parents who received public assistance were awarded child support, while 68% of those who were owed child support payments actually received child support payments.[6]

Table 2. Demographic Characteristics of Custodial Parents by Child Support Award and Receipt Status, 2009 (numbers in thousands)

				Custodial Parents Who Received at Least Some Child Support in 2009		
	Total	% Awarded Child Support	Total Due Child Support	% of Those Due Child Support	Average Child Support ($)	Average Income ($)
All custodial parents	13,672	50.6	5,897	70.8	5,135	31,991
Sex						
Male	2,435	30.4	619	72.9	4,202	42,288
Female	11,237	54.9	5,278	70.5	5,248	30,018
Race and Ethnicity						
White (non-	7,127	55.8	3,410	72.8	5,680	34,961
Hispanic)						
Black	3,439	44.6	1,295	62.1	3,061	28,368
Hispanic	2,662	44.4	1,004	72.7	5,797	25,554
Marital Status						
Married	2,515	52.5	1,152	74.9	4,575	33,979
Divorced	4,589	59.3	2,388	72.9	6,495	37,187
Separated 1,	679	41.6	529	66.9	4,528	25,386
Never married	4,737	44.2	1,763	65.8	3,679	24,901
Educational Attainment						
No high school diploma	1,998	42.2	708	58.9	3,292	14,145
High school graduate	4,555	46.7	1,796	72.9	4,572	24,853
Some college—no degree	3,260	54.7	1,554	70.1	5,448	27,257
Associate's degree	1,565	55.7	735	69.3	6,225	35,951
Bachelor's degree or more	2,279	56.0	1,105	76.8	5,854a	55,458
Economic Characteristics						
Family income below 2009 poverty level	3,876	47.0	1,524	66.3	3,909	8,642
Worked full-time, year-round	6, 772	52.3	3,078	71.8	4,712	44,634
Received public assistance	5,149	48.5	2,093	67.9	4,313	15,412

Source: Table prepared by the Congressional Research Service (CRS) based on data from the U.S. Census Bureau, Current Population Survey, April 2010.

[a] Despite the apparent anomaly (i.e., persons with a B.A. degree received less child support, on average, than persons with a A.A. degree), the average child support amount shown for custodial parents with an A.A degree is not statistically different from the average child support amount shown for custodial parents with a B.A. degree.

Of the categories of custodial parents presented in *Table 2,* custodial parents who were divorced followed by custodial parents who had at least a bachelor's degree were the categories of parents most likely to be *awarded* child support. In 2009, 59.3% of divorced custodial parents and 56.0% of custodial parents with at least a bachelor's degree were awarded child support. The table also shows that custodial parents with at least a bachelor's degree who were owed/due child support were the category of parents most likely to *receive* child support payments in 2009. In 2009, 76.8% of custodial parents with at least a bachelor's degree who were owed payments actually received child support payments. In 2009, the average yearly child support payment received by custodial parents with payments was $5,135; $5,248 for mothers and $4,202 for fathers. These full or partial payments represented 16% of the custodial parent's yearly income, 17% of the custodial mothers' total yearly income, and 10% of the custodial fathers'.

In 2009, for custodial parents with income below the poverty level, child support payments for those who received them made up, on average, 45% of their yearly income. In 2009, child support payments made up 23% of the yearly income of custodial parents without a high school diploma who were owed child support and who actually received full or partial payments. In 2009, child support represented 21% of the income of the 2.4 million custodial parents who received all of the child support that they were owed.[7]

The Census Bureau data also include information on health insurance. In 2009, about 52% of the 6.9 million custodial parents with child support awards had awards that included health insurance. The noncustodial parent provided the health insurance coverage in 44.1% of the awards with health insurance provisos and in 11.7% of the awards without health insurance stipulations. Moreover, the noncustodial parent provided health insurance coverage for 18% of the nearly 6.8 million custodial parents who did not have a child support award.[8] Overall, 3.1 million noncustodial parents provided health care for their children in 2009.[9] This represented 22.8% of the 13.7 million children under age 21 who were living with a custodial parent while their other parent lived elsewhere.

End Notes

[1] U.S. Census Bureau, Custodial Mothers and Fathers and Their Child Support: 2009. Current Population Reports, P60-240, by Timothy S. Grall, December 2011, http://www.census.gov/hhes/www/childsupport/cs09.html. To view detailed tables, see same webpage and click on 2009 detailed tables icon.

[2] It is not surprising that the amount of child support received based on Census bureau data is less the amount of child support collected based on state CSE data because custodial parents responding to the Census survey are often unaware of child support received by the state on their behalf if they are recipients of the Temporary Assistance for Needy Families (TANF) program. In other words, the amount of child support received by TANF parents is probably underreported because many states retain some or all of the child support collected on behalf of such families.

[3] Note that the OCSE defines a CSE "case" as a noncustodial parent (mother, father, or putative/alleged father) who is now or eventually may be obligated under law for the support of a child or children receiving services under the CSE program. If the noncustodial parent owes support for two children by different women, that would be considered two cases; if both children have the same mother, that would be considered one case. Thus, the CSE program caseload may be larger than the national number of custodial parents potentially eligible for child support payments.

[4] Conversely, the reader should note that many custodial parents do not receive child support. In 2009, this included 49% of custodial parents who were not awarded child support and nearly 13% of custodial parents who did not receive any child support payments even though they had been awarded child support. In 2009, this number amounted to almost 8.5 million custodial parents. Some of the reasons given as to why there was not a legal child support obligation included the following: the other parent provided what he or she could (34%); they did not feel the need to make it legal (32%); the other parent could not afford to pay (29%); they did not want the other parent to pay (21%); the child stayed with the other parent part of the time (18%); they could not locate the other parent (17%); they did not want to have contact with the other parent (17%); and paternity was not legally established (8%).

[5] This amount reflects total child support payments received divided by the number of parents who were owed/due payments ($21,400,000,000/5,897,000=$3,634—total different because of rounding). Table 2 shows an average child support payment of $5,135 for custodial parents who actually received at least one child support payment in 2009 ($21,400,000,000/4,174,000=$5,127—total different because of rounding).

[6] Public assistance program participation includes receiving at least one of the following: Medicaid, food stamps, public housing or rent subsidy, Temporary Assistance for Needy Families (TANF), or general assistance.

[7] See Table 6 at http://www.census.gov/hhes/www/childsupport/chldsu09.pdf (p. 17 of 50).

[8] 8 U.S. Census Bureau, Custodial Mothers and Fathers and Their Child Support: 2009, Current Population Reports, P60-240, by Timothy S. Grall, December 2011, http://www.census.gov/hhes/www/childsupport/cs09.html (p. 11) or Table 8 of the detailed tables, http://www.census.gov/hhes/www/childsupport/chldsu09.pdf (p. 35 of 50).

[9] In 2009, nearly 1.6 million noncustodial parents provided health care insurance in cases where it was stipulated in the child support agreement, 0.3 million provided health care insurance in cases were it was not required by the agreement, and 1.2 million provided health care insurance in cases where there was no child support agreement.

In: Child Support Issues
Editor: Rene Pellerin

ISBN 978-1-62808-376-7

Chapter 4

CHILD CUSTODY AND SUPPORT: FREQUENTLY ASKED QUESTIONS*

Alison M. Smith

SUMMARY

Under the U.S. Constitution, Congress has little direct authority to legislate in the field of domestic relations. Generally, state policy guides these decisions.

Despite the lack of direct authority to legislate domestic relations issues, Congress continues to enact federal laws that indirectly affect family law questions concerning child custody and support. This report answers questions frequently asked regarding the interplay between federal and state laws governing these areas.

* This is an edited, reformatted and augmented version of a Congressional Research Service publication, CRS Report for Congress RS21091, prepared for Members and Committees of Congress, from www.crs.gov, dated August 17, 2012.

If Parents Separate and One Parent Moves Out-of-State with Children Before Divorce Proceedings Begin, Where Will Child Custody Issues Be Decided?

A court handling an interstate child custody dispute must consider whether it has jurisdiction to decide the custody case. Three laws provide the answer as to whether a particular court has jurisdiction: the Parental Kidnapping Prevention Act [PKPA],[1] the Uniform Child Jurisdiction and Enforcement Act [UCJEA][2] and the Uniform Child Custody Jurisdiction Act [UCCJA],[3] which has been enacted in some form in all fifty states and the District of Columbia.[4]

The PKPA gives priority to the child's home state (the state where the child lived with at least one parent for six months before the custody petition was filed).[5] If one parent moves with the child to live in a new state, the original state continues to be the home state for an additional six months after the move. The child need not be physically present in the original state for the child custody proceeding to be initiated there by the parent who remained behind.

Can a Custody Order Be Modified?

Yes. In all states, custody orders can be modified by a court to further the best interests of the child.[6] Usually, the parent requesting the modification must convince a judge that a substantial change in circumstances affecting the child's welfare has occurred since the original custody order was entered.[7]

If One Parent Takes a Child to Another State and Tries to Modify Custody There, Which State Will Decide the Case?

Under the PKPA, the court that issued the initial custody decree has "continuing jurisdiction" over custody matters, provided that the first state meets three preconditions: (1) it entered its initial custody order in accordance with the Parental Kidnapping Prevention Act; (2) the child or one parent continues to live in the state; and (3) the state's own law allows continuing jurisdiction.[8]

If these conditions are met, a parent living in another state who wants to modify the initial custody arrangement must file the modification petition in the first state. The UCCJA provides that dismissal is mandatory where the noncustodial parent violates an existing custody order by refusing to return the child to the custodial parent at the end of the child's period of visitation and then asks the out-of-state court to modify custody.[9]

Neither the PKPA, UCJEA nor the UCCJA totally precludes the second state from ever modifying the initial custody order. The PKPA permits the second state to modify the initial custody provision if: (1) the second state has jurisdiction to make a child custody determination and (2) the first state no longer has jurisdiction or has declined to exercise jurisdiction.[10]

What Recourse Does a Left-Behind Parent Have in an Interstate Custody Dispute?

The remedies available under the UCJEA and UCCJA are unavailing if the left-behind parent is unable to find the abducting parent and the child. For this reason, the PKPA makes the federal Parent Locator Service available to assist local police in locating the abductor. The PKPA also provides that any state that treats parental kidnapping as a felony may enlist the F.B.I.'s assistance under the federal Fugitive Felon Act in locating the abducting parent, provided he or she has left the state.[11]

Is It a Crime for a Parent to Kidnap a Child?

In many states, parental kidnapping (also known as interference with parental custody) is a felony, depending upon the circumstances.[12] In others, it is a felony if the child is taken from the state.[13] However, in most states, there can be no kidnapping unless there is an existing custody order that the parent has intentionally violated.

Because many parental kidnappings take place before a final custody decree is entered, a few states have extended criminal sanctions to kidnappings that occur before the final custody decree.[14] Several states also permit the court to assess expenses incurred in returning the child against any person convicted of violating the state's criminal custodial interference law.[15]

Parents, although they are subject to the PKPA, remain exempt from criminal sanctions under the general federal kidnapping statute.[16] International parental kidnapping is a federal crime, punishable by a fine and/or imprisonment for up to three years.[17]

WHAT RECOURSE DOES A PARENT HAVE IF THE OTHER PARENT ABDUCTS THE CHILDREN AND TAKES THEM TO ANOTHER COUNTRY?

Once the child has been located, a possible solution to the abduction may be provided by the Hague Convention on the Civil Aspects of International Child Abduction.[18] The Convention is in force in approximately 40 countries, including the United States,[19]

Mexico, Canada, and most of Europe. The countries that have signed the Hague Convention have agreed that a child who is habitually a resident in one country and who is removed to or retained in another country in breach of the left-behind parent's custody rights must be promptly returned to the country of the child's habitual residence.[20] However, the Convention is inapplicable if the child has been abducted to a country that has not signed the Convention or the child is sixteen or older.

Although there need not be a custody decree to invoke the Convention, the left-behind parent must be able to prove that he or she is exercising a "right of custody"[21] at the time of abduction and that he or she had not given permission for the child to be removed or to be retained in the foreign country beyond a specified, agreed-upon time. In the absence of a formal custody order, custodial rights are determined by state law.

It is important to remember that a Hague Convention proceeding is not a custody case. At a hearing under the Hague Convention, the judge's job is to determine only where the custody hearing should take place, not who is entitled to custody of the child.[22]

The goal of the Hague Convention is the child's swift return to his or her original country where the custody dispute can then be resolved, if necessary, in that country's courts.

WHO IS OBLIGED TO PAY CHILD SUPPORT?

Parents are obliged to pay child support whether or not they were ever married. Parents also have an obligation to support all of their children, not just the children who reside with them. Thus, although the noncustodial parent is married to someone else or supporting other children, he or she has a continuing obligation to support the children of a previous marriage or relationship.[23]

CAN CHILD SUPPORT BE WITHHELD FROM AN OBLIGATED PARENT'S PAYCHECK?

Yes. As of January 1, 1994, the Family Support Act of 1988 requires that all new child support orders provide for automatically withholding child support payments from the obligated parent's paycheck, regardless of whether or not support payments are late.[24]

Federal law permits an exception to immediate withholding if the court finds good cause or if the parents both agree to another arrangement.[25] However, a parent who falls at least one month behind in support payments is subject to withholding even in these cases.[26]

Withholding may be used to collect current support payments as well as arrearages. States have the option, under federal law, to apply withholding to income other than wages and to order withholding from bonuses, commissions, retirement benefits, rental or interest income, or unemployment compensation benefits.[27]

MAY A CHILD SUPPORT ORDER BE MODIFIED?

Yes. States permit a child support order to be modified upward or downward based on proof of a substantial change in the parents' financial circumstances or the child's needs. In addition, federal law requires that child support orders be reviewed every three years unless neither parent requests a review or, in temporary assistance for needy families [TANF] cases, if the review would not be in the child's best interest.[28]

However, child support orders may only be modified prospectively. The 1986 Bradley amendment to the federal child support laws effectively bars retroactive modification that would wipe out past-due support obligations.[29]

ARE THERE CRIMINAL PENALTIES FOR FAILURE TO PAY CHILD SUPPORT?

Yes. A parent who willfully refuses to comply with a lawful order of child support, though able to do so, may be held in contempt of court and jailed or fined for a fixed period of time as punishment or for an indefinite period until the child support is paid.[30]

As of October 1992, failure to pay child support in the interstate context has become a federal crime.[31] An out-of-state parent who has willfully failed to pay court-ordered child support for at least one year or who is at least $5,000 in arrears may be criminally prosecuted by the local United States attorney. For a first offense, the penalties include a fine and/or a prison sentence of up to six months in prison; for a second offense, the punishment is a fine and/or up to two years in jail.

WHAT IF THE CUSTODIAL PARENT DOES NOT KNOW WHERE TO FIND THE NONCUSTODIAL PARENT?

A custodial parent who needs to obtain or enforce a child support order but who cannot find the noncustodial parent may enlist the assistance of a child support enforcement agency run by the state or local government, known as a IV-D agency.[32] This assistance is available to all custodial parents, regardless of whether or not they receive public assistance.[33]

End Notes

[1] 28 U.S.C. §1738A.

[2] 9 U.L.A. 649 (1999 & Supp. 2001). The UCCJA and UCCJEA are only effective to the extent that states adopt them. The UCCJEA has been adopted in some form in 27 states with pending legislation in nine other states.

[3] 9 U.L.A. pt. 1, 262-63 (1999 & Supp. 2001).

[4] For background information on the relationship between federal and state law, see CRS Report RL31201, Family Law: Congress's Authority to Legislate on Domestic Relations Questions, by Alison M. Smith.

[5] It must be noted that the PKPA does not confer jurisdiction on the federal courts. This act merely delineates which jurisdiction may modify child support and custody orders. As such, the PKPA is inapplicable to intrastate disputes and only relevant in interstate disputes when the jurisdictions have conflicting laws. The jurisdictional guidelines set forth in the PKPA supersede any conflicting state law. As such, parents are bound by state court decisions regarding custody, visitation and support.

[6] Numerous factors converge and influence this standard, including the home environment, stability of the parents, the time a parent and child spend together, the quality of the relationship between parent and child, sexual conduct and criminal background of the parents, as well as other factors the court deems appropriate.

[7] See, e.g., Ward v. Ward, 611 N.E.2d 167 (Ind. App. 1993); Blotske v. Leidholm, 487 N.W.2d 607 (N.D. 1992). But see McMillen v. McMillen, 602 A.2d 845 (Pa. 1992).

[8] 28 U.S.C. §1738A(c).

[9] UCCJA §8(b).

[10] 28 U.S.C. §1738(h).

[11] 18 U.S.C. §1073.

[12] See e.g., Mo. Stat. §565.153 (classifying parental kidnapping as a class D felony); Conn. Gen. Stat §53a-97 (classifying custodial interference as a class D felony if the child or person is removed from the state).

[13] See e.g., Mo. Stat. 565.150 (classifying interference with custody as a class D felony if a person is taken from the state).

[14] See, e.g., Tex. Penal Code Ann. §25.03(a)(2).

[15] Minn. Stat. Ann. §609.26, subd. 4; Ind. Code §35-42-3-4(e). See Vanness v. State, 605 N.E.2d 777 (Ind. App. 1992).

[16] 18 U.S.C. §1201(a).

[17] 18 U.S.C. §1204.

[18] For additional information on this topic, see CRS Report RS21261, International Parental Child Abductions, by Alison M. Smith.

[19] Congress passed the International Child Abduction Remedies Act in 1988 to implement the Convention. See 42 U.S.C. 11601 et seq.

[20] The term habitual residence is left undefined by the Hague Convention. Courts have struggled to define it. See Friedrich v. Friedrich, 983 F.2d 1396 (6th Cir. 1993); Levesque v. Levesque, 816 F. Supp. 662 (D. Kan. 1993).

[21] The Convention defines right of custody as including "rights relating to the care of the person of the child and, in particular, the right to determine the child's place of residence." See Hague Convention, art. 5(a), 19 I.L.M. 1501 (1980). A left-behind parent who lacks physical custody of the child may nonetheless have a custody right if there is an outstanding custody order requiring that parent to consent to a relocation of the child. But see Viragh v. Foldes, 612 N.E.2d 241 (Mass. 1993)(visitation is not a right of custody).

[22] Tahan v. Duquette, 259 N.J. Super. 328, 613 A.2d 486 (1992).

[23] See generally, Roger J.R. Levesque, Targeting "Deadbeat" Dads: The Problem With The Direction of Welfare, 15 HAMLINE J. PUB. L. & POL'Y 1, 10-11 (1994)(discussing the financial responsibilities of custodial and noncustodial parents).

[24] 42 U.S.C. §666(a)(1) and 666(b) and 45 C.F.R. §303.100.

[25] 42 U.S.C. §666(a)(8)(B)(i); 42 U.S.C. §666(b)(3).

[26] 42 U.S.C. §666(b)(3)(B).

[27] 42 U.S.C. §666(b)(8)(giving states the option of extending withholding to income other than wages); 45 C.F.R. §302.65 (withholding of unemployment compensation). Also, passports may be denied, revoked, or restricted for individuals certified by a state agency as owing more than $2,500 in past due support. 42 U.S.C. 652(k) and 22 C.F.R §§51.70(a)(8), 51.72(a) and 51.80(a)(2). The Deficit Reduction Act of 2005 (P.L. 109-171) reduced the arrearage amount from $5,000 to $2,500.

[28] 42 U.S.C. §666(a)(10)(A)(i).

[29] 42 U.S.C. §666(a)(9).

[30] See e.g. N.Y. Fam. Ct. §454 (listing possible punishments including suspension of driving privileges, imprisonment for a term not to exceed six months). For further information, see CRS Report R42389, Child Support Enforcement: Incarceration As the Last Resort Penalty For Nonpayment of Support, by Carmen Solomon-Fears, Alison M. Smith, and Carla Berry.

[31] 18 U.S.C. §228.

[32] These state and local agencies are known as IV-D agencies in reference to Title IV-D of the Social Security Act, which governs state enforcement of child support for the recipients of public assistance and which requires states to assist custodial parents in locating support obligors and in obtaining and enforcing support orders.

[33] Custodial parents who receive public assistance or Medicaid can get this help for free. Others who want help may be asked to pay an application fee (which may not exceed $25) as well as a small additional charge if the state needs to use the Federal Parent Locator Service for help in finding the obligor. See 45 C.F.R. §302.33 (availability of IV-D services to individuals not receiving public assistance).

INDEX

D

E

F

G

H

N

O

P

Q

R

S

T

U

V

W

X